CONIECTANEA BIBLICA · OLD TESTAMENT SERIES 12

INGER LJUNG

# TRADITION
# AND INTERPRETATION

*A Study of the Use and Application of Formulaic
Language in the so-called Ebed YHWH-psalms*

CWK GLEERUP LUND SWEDEN

ISBN 91-40-04669-9

CWK Gleerup is the imprint for the scientific and
scholarly publications of Liber Läromedel Lund

Printed in Sweden by
Almqvist & Wiksell, Uppsala 1978

# CONTENTS

**Abstract**

Ljung, I. 1978. Tradition and interpretation. A Study of the Use and Application of Formulaic Language in the so-called Ebed YHWH-psalms. *Coniectanea Biblica*, Ser. 12. 144 pp. Uppsala. ISBN 91-40-04669-9.

The point of departure for any investigation of Old Testament texts concerning form, function, motifs, etc., should be the texts themselves. The present work is centered around the problem of the applicability of formulaic language in the attempts to establish a common Gattung for a number of psalms. The isolation of formulas and formulaic systems with similar function in similar contexts provides a formally related group of texts. The structures of these texts are compared, and a basic compositional pattern is deduced.

Formulas and formulaic systems are found to express general ideas, whereas non-formulaic sections indicate special situations. Non-formulaic sections describing personal misery and/or displaying a paradigmatic understanding and plural applications of the accounts of individual salvation show motifs similar to those contained in Deutero-Isaiah, Job, and Lamentations. Such sections, showing a common "Horizont", deviating from that of the units conforming to the compositional pattern, are seen as the result of an exilic/post-exilic re-reading (Neuinterpretation) of traditional individual laments. In their present form the suffering-, or Ebed YHWH-psalms, reflect the situation after the fall of Judah rather than the cultic function of the sacral king in the Annual Festival.

*Inger Ljung. Faculty of Theology, Department of OT, Uppsala University. Box 2006, S-750 02 Uppsala, Sweden.*

7

# ABBREVIATIONS

I.1: Abbreviations for word classes.

a. N    a nominal, i.e. a noun or any structure that can take the place of a noun in a syntactical structure.

   n    noun.

   adj    adjective.

   ptc    participle.

   pr    pronoun.

   rel    relative pronoun.

   s    final suffix.

   DN    divine name, standing for "YHWH", "Elohim", "El", "Adonai", or any other of the proper names referring to YHWH. Final suffixes often attached to many of these words are not indicated.

b. V    a verbal, i.e. a verb or any structure that can substitute for a verb in a syntactical structure.

   v    verb. On a number of occasions a verb will be identified simply as "perf" for perfect, "impf" for imperfect, or "impv" for imperative. The person, gender, and number may also be given, e.g. "3 m sg" for third masculine singular.

c. vn    verbal noun (the so-called infinitive construct). A verbal noun has some of the functions of a noun and some of the functions of a verb. Consequently, in the descriptions of the patterns, it can be considered a nominal when it stands where a noun can stand and it can be considered a verbal when it takes verbal modifiers.

d. Part    particle, i.e., words that do not fit into the classes of nominals, verbals, or verbal nouns.

   p    preposition.

   adv    adverb. This classification includes all such particles as time words, place words, clause modifiers, and verbal modifiers not separately identified.

   neg    negative.

   inter    interrogative. (Culley, 1967: 34 f.)

I.2: Arbitrary signs.

    −   joins morphemes within the limits of the word, such as inseparable prepositions, final suffixes, and the conjunction <u>waw</u>.

    +   stands between two elements, the first of which is bound to the second to make a "bound structure" (construct relationship).

    x   marks a position in a pattern in which there is free substitution, i.e., where different word classes or constructions have been substituted (Culley, 1967: 35).

II   Other abbreviations follow those established for *Theologisches Wörterbuch zum Alten Testament* (periodicals) and the *Jerusalem Bible* (the books of the Bible). The English quotations are, when not otherwise stated, taken from the *Jerusalem Bible*.

# INTRODUCTION

The similarities of motif between Deutero-Isaiah and a number of Psalms have long been recognized; in particular the close relationship between the Servant Songs and a number of mainly individual laments has been underlined. Adducing extra-biblical comparative material to their discussion of these texts, scholars have suggested that they pertain to the Annual Festival; by identifying the (suffering) subject with the sacral king one has also meant that they functioned as rituals or reflections of rituals. These specifications of "Sitz im Leben" and function have led to the isolation of a particular "Gattung", comprising a number of suffering-psalms—so called Ebed YHWH- or "through death to life"-psalms.

Specification of genre on the grounds of motif-analysis alone involves however a number of problems; nevertheless, motifs are realized in a specific language, and this language can be subjected to formal description, analysis, and comparison, and such a procedure can then provide criteria for establishing "Form" (shape) and function.

The preliminary limitation of a group of psalms which is held together by a common use of formulaic language is my starting point in asking whether the proposed Ebed YHWH-complex exists or not; by describing the distribution and application of such set expressions in their contexts I arrive at a group of formulas and formulaic systems with similar function in similar contexts; furthermore, a number of expressions transpire, for which no set correlation between phrase and context can be established.

By starting with the smaller formulaic elements within a literary unit and then expanding the perspective to other formally similar units, I should be one step closer to the isolation of a complex signified by a common "Horizont". Formulaic similarities alone do not however provide criteria for "Gattungsbestimmung", but should be coupled with structural similarities, and thus my next step is an attempt to establish a structural pattern, common to a group of psalms.

Applying A. B. Lord's (1974: 43) observations that "the phrases for the ideas most commonly used become more securely fixed than those for less frequent ideas", I suggest that there existed a convention for the composition of individual laments with exhortations, short motivations, and pledges

11

securely fixed, i.e. realized in formulaic language. Prolonged motivations, which mainly lack such set language, appear to have been moulded to fit special situations.

The determination of a "Sitz im Leben" or a cultural background of the group(s) isolated can only follow upon the "Gattungsbestimmung", and can only be based on the analysis of formulaic language, as the use of set phrases is probably not arbitrary but points back to a specific sphere of thought.

Substantial sections within the formulaic psalms are however devoid of formulaic language and show indications of a "Horizont" differing from that of the units conforming to the compositional convention; in these sections an analysis of the most frequent motifs is the only means of determining their cultural background.

Only after one has attempted to establish "Form", function and cultural background in this manner, extra-biblical comparative material could be used to shed light on the investigated texts—the results of this study do however make this procedure superfluous.

# A. BACKGROUND

1. Interpreting Ps. 89 A. R. Johnson makes the identification king/Messiah—suffering Servant of the Lord:

". . . the Davidic king, for all that he is the specially chosen servant of the omnipotent King, is a suffering Servant. He is the Messiah of Yahweh; but on this occasion, at least, he is a humble Messiah. What we see, however, is a ritual humiliation in principle not unlike that suffered by the Babylonian king in the analogous New Year Festival."[1] (Cf. also p. 107 ff. on Ps. 18.)

2.1. In his article on "suffering" in Swedish Biblical Encyclopedia[2] I. Engnell deals with a group within the Book of Psalms, more specifically a rather large group of 'royal passion psalms', laments and invocations, often so called psalms of confidence. These psalms in their original setting pertain to the royal cult and to the rôle of the king as subject to vicarious suffering.

. . . This group often contains an elaborate account of distress, a detailed and colorful description of the suffering to which the psalmist has been, or is, subject. In connexion with this there is frequently a presentation of the enemy (-ies). The suffering is described as occasioned by certain enemies, who, along with the suffering itself, are depicted in strong colors and represented in magical categories, not only as evildoers, etc., but also as demonic figures in the guise of different animals, such as dogs, lions, wild bulls, etc. (cf. especially Ps. 22: 13 ff.). The suffering is often described as illness or a condition which resembles illness: the limbs are withered away, the bones are crushed, etc. But the suffering never consists of exclusively physical phenomena—even the soul is distressed: it pines away, dries up, is dissolved, etc. In addition, the suffering is described as imprisonment, as a binding of hands and feet, and, above all, as an already realized or imminent descent into, and sojourn in, the realm of death.

. . . It is the hostile, ever lurking powers of chaos, which in different manifestations threaten the pious community, i.e. the people, and their leader, the sacral king. This is especially true of a number of suffering-psalms belonging to the group characterized as 'royal passion psalms', such as Pss. 18, 22, 49, 88, 116, 118, etc.

13

...The king appears in these psalms as the suffering Servant of the Lord, fighting the powers of chaos—in cult and ideology represented at the same time by mythical powers and actual (national) enemies, all of them depicted in magical-demonic categories. At first he succumbs, is beaten and lacerated, punished on behalf of his people, whose sin/guilt he bears (so called psalms of innocence with 'negative confession') but expiates through his vicarious suffering, which culminates in his 'descent into Sheol'.

Here, in the drama of the Annual Festival, we have the cultic setting to which a number of the most important suffering-psalms belong. From this setting we also understand the cosmic proportions of the misery and suffering. And here we find the explanation of the sojourn in the realm of death which so often concludes the description of suffering: the liturgical subject of the psalm, i.e., in the original setting, the king, is imprisoned, bound in the fetters of death, washed over by the surges of Sheol, encompassed in its darkness: 16:10, 18:5, 17, 28:1, 30:1ff., 39:14, 49:16, 69:1ff., 15f., 86:13, 88:4ff., 89:49, 116:8, 118:8, etc.

... But here, in the realm of death, he keeps his confidence and hope, knowing that his suffering will have an end, that victory will follow, and that resurrection is within reach for him. Being righteous, he knows that YHWH will deliver him from distress and tribulation, break the bonds of death and restore him to the land of the living along with his people, his congregation, which he has redeemed through his suffering and death.

... It should be observed, however, that with this interpretation of the original setting of these psalms, we have not answered the question of their *actual* application, use and interpretation in the course of time.

... At any rate, it is characteristic that the traditional ideology persists with unabated intensity through the centuries. This becomes apparent if we focus our interest on the Ebed YHWH-figure in Second Isaiah, the Suffering Servant of the Lord in Is. 40–55—particularly the so called fourth Ebed YHWH-song in Is. 52:13–53:12, the most important text of the OT.

2.2. Discussing the aspect of suffering in Deutero-Isaiah, Engnell also refers to a number of psalms displaying motifs similar to those found in the Servant Songs: "the said psalms (18, 22, 49, 116, etc.) are—in accordance with the cultic interpretation of the Book of Psalms—to be judged as rituals, directly referring to the cultic function of the sacral king. The Ebed YHWH-songs, on the other hand, must be characterized as prophetic "Nachdichtung" from a liturgical collection pertaining to the Annual Festival".[3]

3. C. Lindhagen lists the following Ebed YHWH-psalms: 18, 49, 88, 89, 116, 118, Is. 38: 9 ff., etc., stating: "The designation pertains to the ideology and original cultic setting of these psalms, not to the term 'servant' which is not present in several of them".[4]

4. In *The Messiah in the Old Testament*[5] and *Israelite Religion*[6] H. Ringgren outlines a series of motifs appearing in a group of psalms, dealing with the theme "Through Death to Life". This group comprises Pss. 18, 22, 69, 71, 86, 88, 116, 118 and the psalm of Hezekiah in Isaiah 38. The following motifs are the most important: "power of death"—"enemies"—"despised"—"saved"—"proclamation of salvation"—"servant-themes" otherwise connected with the New Year, or enthronement, festival–"aid in the morning". The conclusion is: "One may imagine that all this reflects a ritual according to which the king has suffered symbolical death and thus has been humiliated for one night and in the morning returned to life and proclaimed his salvation to the people gathered for the Festival.

. . . But as long as we have only the psalms as our source all this must remain a hypothesis. But this much is certain, that there has existed in Israel a pattern of (innocent) suffering, death and restoration, and that psalms built on this pattern on some occasions have been laid in the mouth of a king (Ps. 18, Is. 38), and, further, that these psalms often contain motifs connected with the Enthronement Festival".[7]

# B. PRELIMINARY PROBLEMS

"Ebed YHWH"-psalms, or "Through Death to Life"-psalms, is a fairly wide designation and no precise criteria are given for defining the group. Working with Engnell's material I encountered the difficulty of distinguishing his postulated complex from "ordinary" individual laments; Ringgren's pattern is an attempt at systematization, but none of the listed psalms contains more than three or four motifs from the pattern—to assume a common ritual background on such a basis alone seems somewhat doubtful.[1]

Motifs are, however, realized in a specific language, and this language can be subjected to formal description, analysis and comparison, which, in turn, can provide criteria for establishing "Form" and function.[2] If certain formal similarities can be ascertained along with the thematic ones, we shall be in a better position to discuss patterns or "Schemata"[3]—if not, we shall be left with an abstraction.

# C. PREMISES

1. A literary critical/historical analysis presupposes a preliminarily limited text; every psalm is therefore considered as a literary unit for the time being.

1.1. Every literary unit exists in a specific form (shape) which also implies specific contents. The isolation of formal, linguistic elements therefore involves definition of these specific contents; the analysis of formal structure precedes the analysis of content.[1]

2. Every literary unit consists of a limited number of smaller units, clauses, or, in the case of poetry, "stanzas"/cola. These smaller units will be the object of a preliminary survey to determine whether phrases, similar in construction and function, are present in the psalms. If so, and if a formally related group emerges, it should be possible to isolate a common "Horizont"[2] for the texts in which such phrases occur.

3. An "author's" use of set phrases is probably not arbitrary but rather indicates a specific sphere of thought.[3] An analysis of set phrases may therefore provide criteria for the isolation of constituents of a cultural background, and, if the phrases appear in a certain order, of "Schemata" given within that background.[4]

# D. DEFINITIONS AND PRELIMINARY LIMITATION

1. In a number of works M. Parry presented his theory that the highly traditional diction of the Homeric poems was in fact oral style;[1] he also developed a system of defining and classifying this traditional diction. Parry's methods were later adopted by other scholars working with traditional literature, most notably A. B. Lord.[2] The works of Parry and Lord have influenced Old Testament study as well.[3] In applying their theories to the biblical Psalms, R. C. Culley reformulated the earlier definitions of the formulas, formulaic systems and phrases of traditional diction to relate them to wider areas of research.[4]

Leaving aside Culley's stress on the oral aspect, I shall make use of his definitions, probably the best available in the field of biblical poetry.[5] At this stage of the investigation I only attempt to describe the "Ausdrucksseite"[6] and survey formal similarities within a group of psalms; the generation and presentation of the expressions will be of minor interest.[7] Culley's definitions and working hypotheses are as follows:

1.1. Formula: "a repeated group of words the length of which corresponds to one of the divisions in the poetic structure, such as the line or the smaller divisions within the line created by some formal division such as the caesura."[8]

1.2. Formulaic system: "a group of phrases having the same syntactical pattern, the same metrical pattern, and at least one major lexical item in common."[9]

1.3. As there is no unanimity among scholars as to the metrical principles of Hebrew poetry[10], certain modifications will, according to Culley, be allowed in formulas if the changes do not disrupt the poetic structure. An increase or decrease in the number of syllables would not necessarily disturb that structure and so additions or omissions of the definite article, final pronominal suffixes, and the (ā)-ending of the imperative and first person of the imperfect would be permissible. Changes of aspect, person, gender and number should also be allowed in formulas.[11]

Within the formulaic systems a noun is usually substituted for a noun, a verb for a verb, etc., but sometimes substitution of words of different classes occurs within the systems. The explanation for this change may be found in the freedom of the number of syllables in the line. Culley calls this phenomenon "free substitution".[12]

2. Working with the above definitions and hypotheses, Culley constructed an "index of set phrases" (1967: 35–91) pertaining to the biblical Psalms. Systematizing Culley's index by registering the distribution of set phrases in the individual psalms, I encountered two main groups characterized by formulaic language; one group which, partly by structure, partly by contents of its constitutional elements, could be conventionally labelled "individual laments",[13] and one "hymn"-group. The former consists of Pss. 6, 9, 18, 22, 25, 26, 27, 28, 30, 31, 35, 38, 40, 54, 61, 69, 71, 86, 88, 102, 109, 116, 119, 140, 142, and 143,[14] the latter contains Pss. 33, 92, 96, 97, and 98. The "individual lament"-group provides a suitable starting point in the quest for a formally related group of psalms.

# E. PRELIMINARY SURVEY OF FORMULAS AND FORMULAIC SYSTEMS

Twenty-six "individual laments" (cf. D 2) contained five or more examples of formulaic language. I now ask: are the set phrases common to all the psalms within the group, or could a subgroup with more specific interrelations be isolated?

The starting point for the survey will be psalms which were designated possible "Ebed YHWH"-psalms (cf. A 1–3), and presented a substantial amount of formulaic language (D 2); as an additional means of control and limitation they must contain the term "ebed". These criteria are fulfilled by Pss. 18,[1] 69, 86 and 116. An inventory will be made of the set phrases of these psalms, and a notation of other units within the Book of Psalms in which the registered phrases appear.

Culley's comments on the passages in question are added to the exposition.

1.1. Ps. 18 (F=Formula, S=Formulaic system)

v. 3: cf. Ps. 144: 2, 91: 2, 28: 7. There is no common pattern but each has a series of nouns with first person singular suffixes, and each has a verb with a preposition with suffix either before or after it.[2]

v. 5a: F 116: 3a; cf. also 18: 6b, which can be put in a system with 18: 5a and 116: 3a, with the last noun as constant lexical item. Possible variant system in 18: 6a and 109: 3a, with some features in common with the above: same forms, and, in 18: 5, 116: 3 and 109: 3 double 'ayin verbs with similar meaning. Possible variant 116: 3b with second noun same as in 18: 6a.[3]

v. 6a: cf. v. 5a.

v. 6b: cf. v. 5a.

v. 7d: S 102: 2b, related system in 88: 3a, 79: 11a and Jon. 2: 8c, with same forms in different order. The verb is the same throughout. Suffix change is permitted.[4]
Cf. also 119: 170a with the same form as the others, the verb being a lexical constant, but with different order.[5]

v. 8a: S 77: 19b–d, 97: 4.

v. 9b: S 50: 3c, 97: 3a.

v. 10a–b: Possible formula 144: 5a–b with verb in different aspect and person.[6]

v. 11c: S 104: 3c.

v. 15a–b: Possibly related 144: 6, with verb in different aspect and person.[7]

v. 18: S 142: 7c–d.

20

v. 18 a: Cf. also 142: 7 c, 143: 9 a, 59: 2 a and 31: 16 b in different aspect.[8]

v. 18 b: F 142: 7 d.

v. 19 b: Possibly related 94: 22 a, with different order.[9]

v. 20 b–c: S 22: 9 c–d.

v. 31 b–c: S Pr. 30: 5.

v. 35 a: F 144: 1 c.

v. 48 b: S 47: 4 a, 144: 2 g.

v. 49 c: S 140: 2 b, 5 b.

v. 50 a: S 35: 18 a, 43: 4 c, 57: 10 a, 71: 22 a; cf. also the system 138: 1 a, 86: 12 a, 9: 2 a and 111: 1 a.


## 1.2. Ps. 69

v. 2 b: S Jon. 2: 6.

v. 5 a: S 38: 20 b; cf. also 69: 5 b.

v. 5 b: cf. also 38: 20 b, 69: 5 a with the same pattern but no common lexical item except the suffix, although the x element in 5 b is the same as in 38: 20 b.[10]

v. 5 a–b: S 40: 13.[11]

v. 6 a: cf. also 69: 20 a, 142: 4 b, 139: 2 a, Jr. 17: 6, with the same pattern and lexical constants, except for lack of preposition before the noun.[12]

v. 17 a: S 6: 3 c, 26: 1 a with related system in 6: 3 a, 31: 10 a, 56: 2 a and 86: 3 a, where the x element is introduced by a particle which is part of the pattern. The structure and lexical content of each clause is different, although each presents a motivation for the prayer expressed in the imperative.[13]

v. 17 b: cf. also 63: 4 a, 109: 21 b.

v. 18 a: cf. 27: 9 a, 102: 3 a, 143: 7 c; as inter 13: 2 b, 88: 15, and in the perfect 22: 25 c.[14]

v. 18 b: cf. also 31: 10 b, Lm. 1: 20.[15]

v. 18 c: S 102: 3 d; cf. also 143: 7 a.[16]

v. 20 a: S 142: 4 b, 139: 2 a, where the nominal is a verbal noun, which can function as a noun substitute, and Jr. 17: 16. Cf. also 69: 6 a.[17]

v. 30 a: S 40: 18 a; variant system in 86: 1 c, 109: 22 a and 25: 16 c.


## 1.3. Ps. 86

v. 1 a–b: Cf. also 31: 3 a, 71: 2 c, 102: 3 a; 88: 3 b, 17: 6 c; in the perfect 116: 2 a. The phrases 31: 3, 71: 2 and 102: 3 are a formula—the other phrases appear to be variations. 88: 3 and 17: 6 are related to the formula in that they have the same imperative and noun with suffix, 116: 2 with added particle.[18]

v. 1 c: S 109: 22 a, 25: 16 c; variant system 40: 18, 69: 30 a.

v. 2 a: S 25: 20 a, 17: 13 d, 120: 2 a; cf. also 6: 5 a, 116: 4 b–c.[19]

v. 3: S 6: 3 a, 31: 10 a, 56: 2 a, related system 6: 3 b, 26: 1 a, 69: 17 a.[20]

v. 3 b: S 61: 3 a, which could be a variation of the formula in 30: 9 a, Jl. 1: 9, because of the preposition with suffix and the verb, which is the same in all the phrases.[21]

v. 4 b: F 25: 1; variation in the perfect with common lexical items in 143: 8 d, 123: 1 a.

v. 6 a: S 55: 2 a, 61: 2 a, also in the perfect in 6: 10 a; 55: 2 and 86: 6 constitute a formula.

v. 6 b: S 140: 7 b, 28: 2 a, also in the perfect in 66: 19 b, 31: 23 c; another variation in the perfect in 6: 9 b, 28: 6 b.

v. 11 a: S 27: 11 a, 119: 33 a.

v. 11 b: (forms part of a colon only) F. 26: 3 b.

v. 12 a: S 138: 1 a, 9: 2 a, 111: 1 a. Cf. also the system 35: 18 a, 43: 4 c, 57: 10 a, 18: 50 a, 71: 22 a, with the same general pattern of verb-nominal-preposition-nominal—verb and preposition the same in each—one may be the variant of the other.[22]

v. 12 b: S 61:9 a, 145:1 b, 2 b, 22:23 a.

v. 13 b: S 56:14 a, 116:8 a.

v. 14: A considerable block of material is repeated in 54:5.

v. 15: F 103:8, Jo. 2:13, in prose Jon. 4:2, Ex. 34:6, Nb. 14:18; variation in Ps. 145:8. Note the following combinations: 86:15 – 103:8 – 145:8 – Jo. 2:13 (– Ex. 34:6 – Jon. 4:2).[23]

v. 16 a–b: F 25:16 a–b, 119:132 a–b.

1.4. Ps. 116.

v. 2 a: cf. also 31:3 a, 71:2 c, 102:3 a, related system 88:3 b, 17:6 c. Cf. also 86:1.[24]

v. 3 a: F 18:5 a, also 18:6 b; possible variant system 18:6 a, 109:3 a; possible variant 116:3 b with the same forms; with double ʿayin verbs in 18:5, 116:3 a and 109:3. The order is different but one may have developed from the other. 116:3 b can be considered a possible variation because the second noun is the same as the second noun in 18:6.[25]

v. 3 b: cf. v. 3 a.

v. 4 b: S 6:5 a, also 25:20 a, 86:2 a, 17:13 d, 120:2 a.[26]

v. 7 b: F 13:6 c–d, 142:8 d.

v. 8 a: S 56:14 a, 86:13 b.

v. 11 a: S 30:7 a, 31:23 a. Cf. also Is. 38:10, Jon. 2:5.

v. 16 a: F 143:12 c.

# 2. Evaluation

2.1. If the number of formulas and formulaic systems characterized by Culley as typical for "individual laments" is compared with the entire population of formulaic language in the Psalms,[27] Pss. 9, 26, and 30 from the starting group (D 2) show less than 75% of their total formulaic language as bound in "individual lament"-phrases; Ps. 18 has exactly 75%.

While these psalms contain a relatively large proportion of "hymnic language", Pss. 6, 25, 27, 28, 38, 54, 61, 69, 88, 109, 116, 119 and 140 entirely lack such terminology.

2.2. In the survey under E 1 some of the psalms from my starting group proved to contain set phrases which were also found in units other than those listed under D 2. Apart from isolated similarities to a number of psalms,[28] four phrases in common with Ps. 17[29], and four with Ps. 56[30] were noted. Furthermore, in a few cases I was referred to Jon. 2:5, 6 and 8, to Jr. 17:16, to Jo. 1:19 and 2:13, to Lm. 1:20, and to Pr. 30:5.

2.3. Starting in Pss. 18, 69, 86 and 116, a number of set phrases were found, common to them and to some of the psalms listed under D 2. When I compared these set phrases with the sum total of the formulaic language of the D 2 units,[31] it appeared that Pss. 9, 18,[32] 27, 31, 35, 38, 40, 54, 71, 119 and 143 had less than one third of their stock of set phrases within the group under E 1; Pss. 22 and 30 had exactly one third.

In order to determine whether this is a coincidence due to arbitrary selection, I introduce a control group, consisting of Pss. 6, 25, 31 and 142—all containing a fairly large number of set phrases.[33] The method of survey will be the same as under E 1.

2.3.1. Psalm 6.
v. 2: S 38: 2.
v. 3a: S 31: 10a, 56: 2a, 86: 3a, related system 6: 3c, 26: 1a, 69: 17a.
v. 3c: cf. 6: 3a.
v. 5a: S 90: 13. Here it appears that a colon has been formed from two smaller elements, which are constants.[34]
v. 5b: S 116: 4b; cf. also 25: 20a–b, 86: 2a–b, 17: 13d, 120: 2a.
v. 5c: S 31: 17b, 109: 26b. In 31 and 109 an inseparable preposition is substituted for the separable in 6: 5.
v. 8a: S 31: 10c.
v. 9b: S 28: 6b. Also in impv 86: 6b, 140: 7b, 28: 2a; other variant in perf 66: 19b.
v. 10a: Also in impv 55: 2a, 86: 6a, 61: 2a.
v. 11a: cf. also 83: 18, where the correspondence of lexical items, forms and structure is only partial. The passages do contain similarities: the first two words in each are the same. The pattern of these two words is the same as the pattern of a system comprising 71: 13a, 35: 4a, 40: 15a and 35: 26a. The phrases in Pss. 6 and 83 may originally have been variants of that system.[35]
(3a, 3c, 5a, 5b are followed by an x-element.)


2.3.2. Psalm 25.
v. 1: F 86: 4b, variation in the perf with common lexical items 143: 8d, 123: 1a.[36]
v. 2a–b: Possible variation of formula in 31: 2a–b, 71: 1—with substitution of verb. Cf. also 25: 20c–d; 16: 1 with free substitution and 143: 8b with different order.[37]
v. 5c: S 31: 5c, 71: 5a, 91: 9a, 143: 10b, 43: 2a. Possible variation with a participle as the nominal and added prepositional phrase in 22: 10a.[38]
v. 16a–b: F 86: 16a–b, 119: 132a–b.
v. 16c: S 86: 1c, 109: 22a.
v. 18a: S 9: 14a with addition of two words; 119: 153a.
v. 20a–b: S 86: 2a, 17: 13d, 120: 2a. Also 6: 5a, 116: 4b.[39]
v. 20c–d: S 16: 1 with possible variation in 143: 8b.[40]
(20a is followed by an x-element).


2.3.3. Psalm 31.
v. 2a–b: F 71: 1, possible variation in 25: 20c–d—a shortened version with substitution of the verb. Cf. also 25: 20c–d, 16: 1, with possible variation 143: 8b, with certain forms and lexical items in common; 143 with different order.[41]
v. 2c: S 119: 40b, variant in impf 71: 2a, possibly related 143: 1c, 54: 3a with the same pattern but no constant major lexical item in common. But the preposition and the suffixes are the same, which suggests that 143 and 54 could be variants created by substitution in both noun and verb positions.[42]
v. 3a: F 71: 3c, 102: 3a, related system 88: 3b, 17: 6c with same impv and noun with suffix— in 17: 6 expanded into a longer colon by the addition of two words. Cf. also 116: 2a, a

23

variation in the perf, and 86: 1 a, with the addition of DN and free substitution in the last position of a verb with suffix instead of a preposition with a nominal.[43]

v. 4 a: S 71: 3 d, 40: 18 c, 119: 114 a.

v. 5 a: S 9: 16 b, with following free substitution.

v. 5 b: S 71: 5 a, 91: 9 a, 143: 10 a, 43: 2 b, 25: 5 c.

v. 7 a: F Jon. 2: 9.

v. 8 a–b: S 118: 24 b–c, Is. 25: 9, variation 90: 14 b–c, cf. also 9: 3 a–b.

v. 10 a: S 6: 3 a, 56: 2 a, 86: 3 a, related system 6: 3 c, 26: 1 a, 69: 17 a.

v. 10 b: S Lm. 1: 20, cf. also Ps. 69: 18 b.

v. 10 c: S 6: 8 a.

v. 11 a: S 102: 4 a.

v. 14 a–b: F Jr. 20: 10.

v. 15 b–c: F 140: 7 a–b, variant systems 142: 6 b–c, 16: 2 a–b.[44]

v. 16 b: S 142: 7 b, 143: 9 a, 59: 2 a, also in impf 18: 18 a.[45]

v. 17 b: S 109: 26 b, 6: 5 c.

v. 21 a: S 61: 5 b, cf. also 17: 8 b, 36: 8 b, 57: 2 d, 63: 8 b with some similarities.[46]

v. 23 a: S 30: 7 a, 116: 11 a, cf. also Is. 38: 11, and 31: 23—Jon. 2: 5.[47]

v. 23 c: F 28: 2. Cf. also S 66: 19, 86: 6 b, 140: 7 b, 28: 2 a and 6: 9 b, 28: 6 b.[48]

v. 23 d: F 28: 2 b.

v. 25 a–b: F 27: 14 b–c.

(10 a contains an x-element).

2.3.4. Psalm 142.

v. 2 a: S 3: 5 a, 142: 2 b.

v. 2 b: S 3: 5 a, 142: 2 a. Related system in 77: 2 a, 77: 2 b beginning with the same words as 3 and 142 but completed differently—in 77: 2 a with a conjunction and impf, in 77: 2 b with a conjunction and impv plus preposition with suffix.[49]

v. 4 a: S 143: 4 a, Jon. 2: 8.[50]

v. 4 b: S 69: 20 a, 139: 2 a, Jr. 17: 16, cf. also 69: 6 a, with the same pattern and lexical constants, except that a preposition precedes the noun.[51]

v. 4 c: S 32: 8 b, variant with verb in place of noun 143: 8 c.

v. 4 d: S 140: 6 a, 119: 110 a.

v. 5 a: S 80: 15 b, Is. 63: 15.

v. 6 a: S 30: 3 a, cf. also 88: 14 a—variations of the formula in 30: 9 a, Jl. 1: 19, Ps. 28: 1 a and related system in 61: 3 c and 86: 3 b.[52]

v. 6 b: S 16: 2 a, cf. also 31: 15 b, 140: 7 a.

v. 7 a: S 143: 1 b.

v. 7 b: F 79: 8 c.

v. 7 c: S 143: 9 a, 59: 2 a, 31: 16 b.

v. 7 c–d: Note the full line system 142: 7 c–d, 18: 18.

v. 8 a: S 22: 21 a, variation in impf 143: 11 b.

v. 8 d: F 13: 6 d, 116: 7 b.[53]

# 3. Evaluation

3.1. Starting in Pss. 6, 25, 31 and 142 a number of set phrases common to them and some of the psalms listed under D 2 were found. When I compared these set phrases with the sum total of the formulaic language of the D 2 units[54] I found that Ps. 9 only had three relevant phrases of the total 13 entries, which is less than one third; this is also true of Pss. 18, 22, 27, 35, 38, 40, 54, 102 and 142.[55]

Psalm 102 shows fewer set phrases in common with Pss. 6, 25, 31, 142 than with Pss. 18, 69, 86, 116. Although the phrases are concentrated to the beginning of the psalm, they are evenly distributed throughout the control groups.

Psalm 28 contains a greater number of set phrases in common with the second control group than with the first, mainly due to formulaic resemblance to Ps. 6 and 31;[56] Pss. 140 and 143 also present an increased proportion of formulaic language.

3.2. In the survey under E 2 my control psalms proved to contain set phrases, which were also found in units other than those listed under D 2. Apart from isolated similarities to a number of psalms,[57] five phrases in common with Ps. 16,[58] four with Ps. 17,[59] and three with Ps. 56[60] were noted. Furthermore, in a few cases I was referred to Jon. 2: 5, 8 and 9, to Is. 25: 9 and 38: 11, to Jr. 17: 16 and 20: 20, to Jo. 1: 19, and to Lm. 1: 20.

# 4. Summary and conclusions

Twenty-six psalms contained five or more instances of formulaic language. Out of such set phrases, 75 % or more could be designated formulas/formulaic systems of "individual laments" in Pss. 6, 18, 22, 25, 27, 28, 31, 35, 38, 40, 54, 61, 69, 71, 86, 88, 102, 109, 116, 119, 140, 142 and 143. To determine whether these psalms might have a common "Horizont", the formulaic references from Pss. 18, 69, 86 and 116 were scrutinized. This resulted in the limitation of a group, consisting of Pss. 6, 18, 22, 25, 26, 28, 30, 61, 69, 86, 88, 102, 109, 116, 140, 142, 17 and 56, with 33 % or more of the formulaic language bound in set phrases common to Pss. 18, 69, 86, and 116. Further control, based on Pss. 6, 25, 31 and 142 resulted in the group 6, 25, 26, 28, 30, 31, 61, 69, 71, 86, 88, 109, 116, 119, 140, 143, 16, 17 and 56. The omission of Pss. 18, 22, 102 and 142 and the addition of Pss. (31), 71, 119, 143 and 16 in this second group as compared with the first should be noted.

Psalm 22 has the main part of its set phrases in the form of variations of formulas or formulaic systems—variations pertaining to units which lie outside the scope of this study, and concentrated to vv. 9–14 and 20–25.[61]

Psalm 102 has formulaic language in common with several psalms in the control groups and shows a remarkably high proportion of formulas; these are, however, concentrated to vv. 2–4.

Psalms 31 and 71 have in common several evenly distributed formulas and formulaic systems. These are also well spread among the psalms of the control groups.

Psalm 119 shares its set phrases mainly with psalms which lie outside the scope of this study; Ps. 143 has a high incidence of formulaic language in common with Ps. 142.

Psalms 16, 17 and 56 were added to the group under D 2. According to Culley's index, Ps. 16 displays only two instances of formulaic language, both in vv. 1–2; one system illustrates free substitution,[62] the other calls for a change of vocalization; Ps. 17 has set phrases evenly distributed throughout, and refers in three of the four systems to psalms with common formulaic language. Ps. 56 has its systems well spread both within the psalm and throughout the control groups. Pss. 9, 27, 35, 38, 40, 54, 89 and 144 had too few set phrases in common with the main group (D 2) to justify a place in the further investigation; Pss. 18 and 142 appear in the control groups and may therefore have been denied their due of attention—further study will determine whether or not these psalms belong to the main group.

Psalms 22, 102, 31, 71, 143, 17 and 56 remain within the scope of this investigation for the time being. An analysis of the set phrases in these psalms will provide further arguments for their inclusion in, or exclusion from, the main group.

As a basis for the analysis of formulaic language I thus have the following preliminary group: Pss. 6, 18, 22, 25, 26, 28, 30, 31, 61, 69, 71, 86, 88, 102, 109, 116, 140, 142, 143, 17 and 56.

# F–H. FORMULAS AND FORMULAIC SYSTEMS

A set phrase can have different functions in different contexts. If the same phrase occurs in different contexts it must be assumed that the formula/system is primary; if there is a set correlation between phrase and context this indicates the "Sitz im Leben" of the expression.[1]

By starting with the smaller formulaic elements within a literary unit, and then expanding the perspective to other formally similar units, I should be one step closer to the isolation of a probable Ebed YHWH-complex signified by a common "Horizont".

Since Culley's index is based partly upon content I have at this stage chosen to follow a different principle of systematization: formulaic statements about the psalmist, his relation to YHWH and a third party will be analyzed first (F), then statements about YHWH, his relation to the psalmist and to a third party (G), and finally statements about a third party and his relation to the psalmist and to YHWH (H). I hope, by so doing, to avoid placing the literary units in set "Gattungen" already from the start.

F 1. Nominal- and verbal clauses without a direct object.

1.1. Two groups of nominal clauses expressed in formulaic language containing first person singular pronouns are present in the material: The first group consists of the system Ps. 86: 1–109: 22–25: 16 with variation in 40: 18–69: 30; the second of the formula 116: 16–143: 12.

1.1.1.  86: 1 c–109: 22 a–25: 16 c with 40: 18 a–69: 30 a
(part n c-n pr with c-pr n c-n)[2]

In Ps. *86* the expression is found at the outset (vv. 1–5;[3] formulaic language in v. 1 a, 1 c, 2 a, 2 b, 3 a, 3 b, 4 b[4]). Exhortations are present in v. 1 a, 1 b, 2 a, 2 c, 3 a, and 4 a, followed by ḵi-clauses describing the character (v. 1 c, 2 b) or activities (v. 3 b, 4 b) of the psalmist (cf. however v. 2 d–e). The section is concluded by a nominal ḵi-clause pertaining to YHWH's attributes.

The expression functions in context as one of several set motivations for one of several (set) exhortations.

In Ps. *109* the expression is found in a section (vv. 21–25),[5] introduced by an exhortation (v. 21 a), which is motivated by an expression of confidence (v. 21 b). The next exhortation (v. 21 c) is followed by a motivation referring to the character of the psalmist (v. 22 a). This second motivation leads up to a detailed description of misery (v. 22 b–25). The commands appear again in v. 26, which is closely connected with v. 27 (w$^e$-), where the undefined category from v. 25 recurs (impf 3 pl). Formulaic language is found in v. 21 b–c, 22 a and 22 b.

The expression provides a motivation in a section with exhortations at the beginning and the end, and leads into a non-formulaic description of misery (in the perf, with the exception of v. 25).

In Ps. 25 the expression is found in a section (vv. 16–21),[6] introduced by a double command (v. 16 a–b), which is motivated by the nominal clause in 16 c, mentioning attributes of the psalmist. v. 17 a describes his condition (perf); 17 b contains another exhortation. Further imperatives are found in v. 18 a, 18 b, 19 a, motivated in v. 19 b–c by references to a (hostile) third party (perf 3 pl). Following the double command of vv. 20 a–b is ki and perf 1sg (v. 20 c–d) and (modal) impf 3 pl–s1sg with another ki and perf 1sg (v. 21). Formulaic language is present in v. 16 a–b, 18 a, 20 a–b, 20 c–d.

In a section, containing eight exhortations (v. 16×2, v. 17×1, v. 18×2, 19×1, v. 20×2) the expression constitutes the first motivation and introduces a short description of misery.

In Ps. 69 the variant expression, introduced by waw,[7] seems to form a contrast to the preceding section, dealing with a third party. v. 30 b contains impf 2sg–s1sg.

Ps. 40 was not included in the starting material, but since the closing verses (14–18) display set phrases in v. 14 b, 15 a, 15 b, the latter part of v. 16, v. 17, v. 18 a, and 18 c (as against two instances in vv. 2–13), these should be further investigated.

The variant expression, introduced by waw, appears to delimit and underline the qualities of the psalmist as compared to a third party, described in negative terms in vv. 15–16, positive in v. 17, and leads into modal impf 3sg, followed by a nominal expression of confidence (v. 18 a), and a negative command (v. 18 b).

In Pss. 40 and 69 the investigated expression seems to contrast with the preceding sections. The nominal clauses introduce verbal clauses containing modal impfa in both cases. Ps. 40: 18 a and 69: 30 a have similar function in context.

In Pss. 25 and 86 the expression provides a motivation for one among many exhortations. In Ps. 25 the nominal clause introduces a short description of the condition of the psalmist (v. 17 a, in the perf), a description with no equivalent in Ps. 86. Ps. 25 contains references to a third party, which are lacking in Ps. 86; the structures of 25: 16–21 and 86: 1–5 are also different—thus, no set correlation between phrase and context can be isolated in these two sections. Ps. 109: 22 a, motivating the preceding exhortation, introduces a substantial, non-formulaic account of distress and is thus placed in a category of its own.

### 1.1.2. 116: 16 b–143: 12 c
(part pr n-s)[8]

In Ps. *116* the expression is found in the latter part of the psalm (vv. 10–18),[9] where the nominal clause (preceded by an exclamation) introduces a section which presents the attributes of the psalmist and accounts for YHWH's activity (v. 16,[10] in the perfect)—this suggests a descriptive or confirmative function of the initial ki.[11]

In Ps. *143* the expression is found in the closing section of the psalm (vv. 10 c–12[12]) preceded by modal impfa and perf 2sg for which the nominal clause is the motivation; this indicates a causal function of the initial ki.

As the expression in Ps. 116: 16 b is found in a section also containing references to YHWH's saving acts (in the perfect), possibly dependent on vv. 7 b–8, while Ps. 143: 12 c constitutes the motivation to wishes concerning salvation, the two expressions do not have similar functions in context.

### 1.2.
The remaining formulaic nominal clauses contain prepositions, and are found in 142: 4–143: 4–Jon. 2: 8; 31: 10–Lm. 1: 20 with 69: 18; 38: 18–51: 5; 59: 17–102: 3.

### 1.2.1. 142: 4 a–143: 4 a–Jon. 2: 8 a.
(V p-s n-s)[13]

In Ps. *142,* v. 4 concludes a description of invocation (vv. 2–4 b[14])—the nominal clause introduces an expression of confidence in the perfect.

In *Jon. 2,* v. 8 seems to be linked to the statements about invocation and divine response in v. 3.[15] The nominal clause is followed by perf 1sg – impf-cons.

The expressions seem to have different functions in different contexts: in Ps. 142, v. 4 a must be interpreted in the present, as salvation is not a fact; in Jon. 2, v. 8 is a review.

### 1.2.2. 31: 10 b–Lm. 1: 20 with 69: 18 b.
(x part n p-s with part n p-s x)[16]

Lm. did not form part of the starting group. The system contains approximately half a colon as constant part. This minimal realization of formulaic language is found in Ps. *31* in a section (10–14),[17] opened by an exhortation, which is motivated by the nominal clause, describing the situation of the psalmist. The nominal clause is followed by a detailed specification of personal misery (v. 10 c–14). Formulaic language is present in v. 10 a, 10 b, 10 c, 11 a, 14 a–b.

In Ps. *69* the expression is found in a section (vv. 17–20, cf. above n. F 7), characterized by exhortations with motivations, both categories mainly in formulaic language (v. 17 a, 17 b, 18 a, 18 b, 18 c, 20 a). In this section the nominal clause constitutes the motivation for the third of six exhortations, and is directly followed by a command. The motivations within vv. 17–20 contain references to the attributes of YHWH, the situation of the psalmist, and to a third party.

The contexts of 31: 10 b and 69: 18 b are of different types; in Ps. 31 the section 10–14 is opened by an imperative, the motivation of which leads into a substantial, non-formulaic description of misery, while Ps. 69: 17–20 is dominated by exhortations with motivations. No set correlation can be established between phrase and context.

1.2.3. 38: 18 b–51: 5 b

(c-n-s p-s adv).[18]

None of the psalms formed part of the starting group.

1.2.4. 59: 17 d–102: 3 b

(p-n n p-s)[19]

Ps. *59* did not form part of the starting group and thus there is no relevant comparative material to Ps. *102:* 3 b.


1.3. Formulaic phrases in the first person sing,[20] which do not explicitly define the relations of the psalmist with YHWH or with a third party, are present in both the perfect and imperfect.

1.3.1. The perfect-group contains the following formulas and formulaic systems: 30: 7–31: 23–116: 11, with Is. 38: 10, and Jon. 2: 5; 79: 8–142: 7; 6: 8–31: 10; 143: 5–77: 6; 55: 5–109: 22; 31: 11–102: 4. Under this heading I also include 119: 136–Lm. 3: 48.

1.3.1.1. 30: 7 a–31: 23 a–116: 11 a, Is. 38: 10 a; Jon. 2: 5 a.

(c pr v p-n-s, c pr v p-N-s; c pr v perf 1sg p n-s).[21]

In Ps. *30* the expression is found in the section (vv. 7–8)[22] which is thought to form a transition from vv. 2–6 to vv. 9–13—both passages contain accounts of divine actions (v. 2–4, 13). v. 7 a introduces a quotation (v. 7 b) with an expression of confidence; confidence is also the theme of

v. 8a (perf 2sg), while v. 8b–c (perf 2sg–perf 1sg) speak of uncertainty. v. 7a introduces a review.

In Ps. *31* the expression is found in the latter part of the psalm, in a section (vv. 22–23, cf. n. F 17), initiated by a "bārūk"-statement, leading up to <u>ki</u> with perf 3sg, describing divine action. v. 23a introduces a quotation (v. 23b), containing an account of former misery (perf 1sg), while v. 23c refers back to the salvation (perf 2sg).

In Ps. *116* the expression is found at the outset of the second part of the psalm (cf. above n. F 9). v. 10a contains a presentation of the psalmist, 10b speaks of misery (perf 1sg); the description of the miserable situation continues in v. 11a (p-n), introducing a quotation in the form of a nominal clause (v. 11b).

In *Is. 38* the expression is found at the outset of the unit in a section characterized as a "lament", and leads up to a command.[23] An account of salvation is given in v. 17 (perf 2sg, and <u>ki</u> with perf 2sg and first sing object). vv. 18–19 lack first person sing references—such references are however found in v. 20 together with first person plural forms.

In *Jon. 2* v. 5 separates two accounts of misery (impf–perf, cf. above n. F 15). v. 5a introduces a quotation (v. 5b), containing an account of former misery, leading up to a wish (v. 5c).

Ps. 30:7, 31:23, 116:11, and Jon. 2:5 are preceded by accounts of divine action in the perfect (cf. 30:2b–4 with 3b in impfcons, 31:22b, 116:7b–8, Jona. 2:3 with 3b in impfcons).

Ps. 30:7a and Jon. 2:5a are found in transitional passages between accounts of invocation and saving (30:3–4 and 11–13, Jon. 2:3 and 7c–8). The transitional sections represent the reflexions of the psalmist in a situation prior to the divine intervention.

The sections incorporating Ps. 31:23a and 116:11a are immediately preceded by accounts of divine action; furthermore, Ps. 31:23a–b is followed by a direct account of divine intervention, Ps. 116:11a–b by an indirect one. In association with such accounts, the expression and the following quotation review a former situation.

Is. 38 does not belong to either of these groups.

1.3.1.2.  79:8c–142:7b
(part v adv)[24]

Ps. *79* did not form part of the starting group, so there is no relevant comparative material to Ps. *142:*7b.

1.3.1.3.  6:8a–31:10c
(v p-n n-s)[25]

In Ps. 6 the expression is found in a section (vv. 7–8),[26] which follows upon the outset (characterized by exhortations and motivations) of the psalm. The motivations contain references to the (miserable) condition of the psalmist (perf)—this condition is further described in vv. 7–8.

In Ps. 31 the expression is found in a section (vv. 10–14, cf. above n. F 17), introduced by an exhortation, followed by ki and a nominal clause— this nominal clause is specified in vv. 10c–14 (perf), describing personal misery.

31: 10c is preceded by an exhortation with motivation, and initiates a description of misery, 6: 8a by a section with exhortations and motivations forming part of a description of misery. Thus the two expressions are found in similar contexts, but differ slightly as to function.

1.3.1.4. 143: 5a–77: 6a
(v n p-n)[27]
Ps. 77 did not form part of the starting group, so there is no relevant comparative material to Ps. 143: 5a.

1.3.1.5. 55: 5a–109: 22b
(n-s v p-n-s)[28]
Ps. 55 did not form part of the starting group, so there is no relevant comparative material to Ps. 109: 22b.

1.3.1.6. 31: 11a–102: 4a
(part v p-n n-s)[29]
For Ps. 31 cf. above F 1.3.1.3.

In Ps. 102 the expression is found in a section at the beginning of the psalm (vv. 2–4/12),[30] containing several exhortations. The motivation (ki and perf) follows in v. 4, which, in turn, leads into a detailed description of personal misery.

31: 11a and 102: 4a are both preceded by exhortations, and found at the beginning of extensive descriptions of misery.

1.3.1.7. 119: 136a–Lm. 3: 48a
(n+n v n-s)[31]
None of the texts formed part of the starting group.

1.3.2. The imperfect-group contains the following formulas and formulaic systems: 15: 5–30: 7–10: 6 with variation in 112: 6; 27: 6–57: 8; 73: 13–26: 6. Under this heading I also include 32: 8–142: 4 with variation in 143: 8.

1.3.2.1. 15: 5d–30: 7b–10: 6b, 112: 6a
(neg v p-N, p-N neg v)[32]

Pss. *15, 10,* and *112* did not form part of the starting group, so there is no relevant comparative material to Ps. *30:* 7 b.

### 1.3.2.2. 27: 6d–57: 8c

(impf 1sg c–impf 1sg)[33]

None of the psalms formed part of the starting group.

### 1.3.2.3. 26: 6a–73: 13b

(v p-n n-s)[34]

Ps. *73* did not form part of the starting group, so there is no relevant comparative material to Ps. *26:* 6a.

### 1.3.2.4. 32: 8a–142: 4c, 143: 8c

(p-n rel v, n rel v)[35]

Ps. *32* did not form part of the starting group.

In Ps. *142* the expression opens a section (vv. 4c–5, cf. above n. F 14), which describes personal misery, and summons YHWH to take heed. The investigated phrase leads into perf 3pl, pertaining to the activity of a hostile third party.

In Ps. *143* the expression is found in a section (vv. 7–10b, cf. above n. F 12) characterized by exhortations and motivations. The investigated phrase qualifies the preceding imperative and is followed by <u>ki</u> and perf 1sg.

No set correlation between phrase and context can be established.

2. Verbal clauses defining the relations between YHWH and the psalmist are present both in the perfect and the imperfect.

2.1. Verbal clauses in perf 1sg with YHWH[36] as object are present in the following formulas and formulaic systems: 31: 2–71: 1 with possible variation in 25: 2, and, in different order, in 25: 20–16: 1 with possible variation in 143: 8; 31: 5–140: 7 with variant system in 142: 6–16: 2; 143: 5–77: 13; Jon. 2: 3–120: 1. Here I shall also include 56: 5–56: 12–26: 1, and 86: 11–26: 3.

2.1.1. 31: 2a–b–71: 1a–b, 25: 2a–b with 25: 20 c–d–16: 1b and 143: 8b

(p-s DN v neg v p-n, p-s v neg v with x part v p-s and part p-s v)[37]

Ps. *16* did not form part of the starting group.

In Ps. *31* the expression precedes a section (vv. 2c–5, cf. above n. F 17) characterized by exhortations with motivations. v. 2a–b stand relatively isolated from the following section, and are seen as a summarizing heading (cf. v. 7b, 15a, 18a).

In Ps. *71* the expression precedes a section (vv. 2–5)[38] characterized by exhortations with motivations. v. 1a–b stand isolated and are seen as the summarizing heading of the psalm.

In Ps. 25 the possible variant is found at the outset of the psalm (vv. 2–3, cf. above n. F 6), preceded by a description of the situation (impf). v. 2a leads into neg impf 3pl, containing an expression of confidence. The following stanza deals with the contrast between two parties (neg impf-impf); the subsequent section (vv. 4–7) is characterized by exhortations.

The variant system in 25: 20 is found in the latter part of the psalm in a section (vv. 16–21, cf. above n. F 6) with exhortations and motivations (cf. above F 1.1.1). v. 20 contains two imperatives, neg impf 1sg, and a verbal (perf 1sg) ki-clause. Here the ki-clause is seen as a motivation for the impf 1sg, rather than for the exhortations. The following stanza, closing the psalm, contains modal impf and ki with perf 1sg-s.

In Ps. 143 the possible variation is found in a section (vv. 7–10 b, cf. above n. F 12) characterized by exhortations and motivations. The expression constitutes the motivation for the third exhortation of the section.

In Pss. 31 and 71 the expressions are not linked with the following sections, but form summarizing headings, so that Ps. 31:2a–b and 71:1 are judged as having similar function.

In Pss. 25[II] and 143 the expression occurs in sections containing exhortations and motivations. The abridged variant in 143:8 constitutes a direct motivation for the preceding imperative, while 25:20d forms the motivation to a verbal clause, expressing confidence (neg impf 1sg), and is followed by modal impf and ki with perf 1sg, closing the psalm. The expressions do not have similar function in context.

Ps. 25:2a–b, found at the outset of the psalm, do not represent a heading or motivation; rather, they form part of a general cluster of expressions of confidence and cannot be included in any of the above isolated groups.


2.1.2. 31:15b–140:7a, 142:6b–16:2a

(perf 1sg DN-s pr, perf pr n-s)[39]

Ps. 16 did not form part of the starting group.

In Ps. 31 the expression is found at the outset of a section (vv. 15–18 b/19, cf. above n. F 17) displaying terminological similarity to vv. 2–5, 6–7, and 8–9. v. 15 consists of a verbal clause (perf 1sg) initiated by waw, and followed by an "'āmarti"-phrase. v. 16a addresses YHWH, and the invocation is continued by the exhortations in v. 16c–17. The section is concluded by neg impf 1sg and ki with perf 1sg–s2sg.

In Ps. 140 the expression is found at the outset of a section (vv. 7–8).[40] v. 7 opens with an "'āmarti"-phrase; v. 7b contains an exhortation with first person sing object, v. 8 has a nominal and a verbal (perf 2sg) clause, addressing YHWH and expressing confidence.

In Ps. *142* v. 6 forms a transition between vv. 4c–5 and vv. 7–8 (cf. above n. F 14). The "'āmarti"-phrase is preceded by perf 2sg p-s DN, and introduces an expression of confidence.

In Pss. 31 and 142 the investigated expressions are preceded by verbal clauses (perf 1sg) and followed by short nominal statements and exhortations. In Ps. 31, vv. 15–18b show similarities to vv. 2c–9, which display terminal traits (vv. 8–9; cf. F 4.2.5, G 5.2.4) v. 15 may be regarded as stating the position of the psalmist (v. 15a)[41] and initiating a review of former circumstances, concluded by neg impf with k̲i̲ and perf 1sg (for more general conclusions cf. G 5.2.4). In Ps. 142, vv. 2–4a describe a situation of invocation (iterative impfa), and lead into perf 2sg (v. 4b); vv. 4c–6 refer to personal misery; vv. 7–8a contain exhortations. The modal understanding of v. 8d (cf. n. 14 *ad loc.*) would mean that the psalm lacks expressions of an accomplished salvation. Thus vv. 4c–8d would be an account of the circumstances which led to the situation described in the opening section.

If this tentative reasoning is correct, then Ps. 31:15b and 142:6b both form part of reviews, and may thus be ascribed similar function in context, while Ps. 140:6–7, preceded by exhortations, show a different structure within the section.

### 2.1.3. 143:5b–77:13a
(v p-n+n-s)[42]

Ps. *77* did not form part of the starting group and so there is no relevant comparative material to Ps. *143:*5b.

### 2.1.4. Jon. 2:3a–b–120:1
(v, p-n p-s, p-DN, c-v)[43]

Ps. *120* did not form part of the starting group, so there is no relevant comparative material to *Jon. 2:*3a–b.

### 2.1.5. 56:5b–c–56:12a–b–26:1c–d
(p-DN v neg impf 1sg)[44]

In Ps. *56*[45] the expression is found in v. 5b–c and 12a–b. v. 5b–c are preceded by exhortations, motivated by references to a third party (vv. 2–3/4), and modal impf 1sg (v. 5a)—the consequences of v. 5b–c are expressed in the latter part of the stanza. v. 12 is preceded by descriptions of a third party (vv. 6–8) and expressions of confidence (vv. 10–11), and followed by a promise (modal impf 1sg), motivated by k̲i̲ and perf 1sg (13–

14 b); the consequences of v. 14 a–b are expressed in the latter part of the stanza.

In Ps. *26*[46] the expression is found in the first stanza. The opening exhortation is motivated by ki and perf 1sg, followed by perf 1sg–neg impf 1sg. v. 1 is seen as a summary of the psalm.

No similarities have been found between the contexts in Pss. 26 and 56. The two realizations of the system in Ps. 56 appear in similar contexts, but two occurrences within one psalm could not provide criteria for isolating formulaic language characterizing a group of psalms.

### 2.1.6. 86: 11 b–26: 3 b

(v p-n-s)

Ps. *26:* 3 b contains perf 1sg, while *86:* 11 b has impf 1sg and "appears to form part of a colon only" (Culley, 1967; 75, no. 106).

2.2. Verbal clauses in impf 1sg with second pers sing object, pertaining to YHWH, are present in the following formulas and formulaic systems: 30: 9–Jo. 1: 19–28: 1 with related system in 61: 3–86: 3– cf. also 142: 6–30: 3 and 88: 14; 25: 1–86: 4 with variation in 143: 8–123: 1.

### 2.2.1. 30: 9 a–Jo. 1: 19 a–28: 1 a with 61: 3 a–86: 3 b and 142: 6 a–30: 3 b and 88: 14 a.

(p-s DN impf 1sg with x p-s impf 1sg and perf 1sg p-s DN and p-s DN perf 1sg)[47]

For Ps. *30* cf. above n. F 22. The expression is found at the outset of the second part of the psalm, and is followed by c-p DN impf 1sg, a double question, and exhortations.

In *Jo. 1* the expression is preceded by a description of the "Day of the Lord" (vv. 15–18) and its effects on a plural category (in the perf). The only reference in the chapter to first person sing is found in v. 19—in the same stanza YHWH is also addressed for the first time; the terminology of the motivation points to vv. 17–18.

In Ps. *28* the expression is found at the outset (vv. 1–2),[48] and leads into a negative command and statements of consequence. v 2 contains another command and describes the invocational situation (p-vn-s).

The realization of the related system in Ps. *61* is found at the outset of the psalm (vv. 2–3 c)[49] and forms part of a specification of the personal situation (locality, *action,* condition), which introduces modal impf 2sg-s1sg with motivations.

The other constituent of the related system, Ps. *86:* 3, is found in the opening section of the psalm (vv. 1–5, cf. above n. F 5). The expression forms one among several motivations (v. 1 c, 2 b, 2 d nominal; 3 b, 4 b verbal with impf 1sg) for one among several exhortations.

A variant in the perf is found in Ps. *142:*6 a (for 142: 6 b cf. above F 2.1.2.). 142: 6 was thought to form a transition between the description of want (v. 4 c–5) and the following exhortations.

Ps. *30:* 3 contains perf 1sg. The expression is found in a section describing salvation (cf. above n. F 22) and leads, within the stanza, into impf cons 2sg–s1sg.

In Ps. *88* the expression initiates a section (vv. 14–19)[50] describing invocational activity (v. 14), and referring to abandonment (v. 15) and misery (vv. 16–19). The section lacks exhortations.

In Ps. 30: 9, 28: 1 and 61: 3 the expressions are preceded or followed by exhortations within sections dealing with situations of invocation at the outset of the psalms, while the contexts of Jo. 1: 19, Ps. 86: 3 b, 30: 3, 142: 6 a, and 88: 14 a vary to such a degree that a comparison of the function of the realizations becomes impossible.

2.2.2. 25: 1–86: 4 b with 143: 8 d–123: 1 a
(p-s DN n-s impf 1sg with p-s perf 1sg n-s)[51]

Ps. *123* did not form part of the starting group.

In Ps. *25* the expression forms part of the summarizing heading (cf. above n. F 6).

In Ps. *86* the expression is one among several motivations for one among several exhortations (cf. above n. F 5).

The variant in the perf in Ps. *143* is found in the section 7–10 b (cf. above n. F 12) as one among several motivations for one among several exhortations.

Ps. 86: 4 b and 143: 8 d have similar function in context, while Ps. 25: 1 stands isolated.


2.3. Modal impf 1sg with nomina having second person sing suffixes as objects are present in the following formulas and formulaic systems: 9: 2, 15–26: 7–73: 28; 5: 8–132: 8; 31: 8–118: 24–Is. 25: 9 with variation in 90: 14— cf. also 9: 3 and 40: 17; 61: 9–86: 12–145: 1, 2–22: 23; Under this heading I also include 59: 17–90: 14–92: 3–143: 8; 35: 18–43: 4–57: 10–18: 50–71: 22; cf. also 138: 1–86: 12–9: 2–111: 1; 35: 28–71: 24; 52: 11–54: 8.

2.3.1. 9: 2 b, 15 a–26: 7 b–73: 28 c
(V n+n-s)[52]

Pss. *9* and *73* did not form part of the starting group, so there is no relevant comparative material to Ps. *26:* 7 b.

2.3.2.  5: 8 b–138: 2 a

(v p n+n-s)[53]

None of the psalms formed part of the starting group.

2.3.3.  31: 8 a–b–118: 24 b–c–Is. 25: 9 e–f with 90: 14 b–c and 9: 3 a–b and 40: 17 a–b

(impf 1 c-impf 1 p-N with impf 1 c-impf 1 p-N and impf 1 c-impf 1 p-N and impf 3pl c-impf 3pl p-N)[54]

Pss. *118, 90, 9* and *Is. 25* did not form part of the starting group, Ps. *40:* 17 contains impf 3pl, so there is no basis for comparison with Ps. *31:* 8 a.

2.3.4.  61: 9 a–86: 12 b–145: 1 b, 2 b–22: 23 a

(impf 1sg n-s p-N)[55]

Ps. *145* did not form part of the starting group.

For Ps. *61* cf. above n. F 49. The expression is preceded by a section (vv. 7–8 with modal impfa), displaying motifs not otherwise found in the psalm. The section vv. 5–6 opens with cohortative clauses (v. 5), motivated by ki and perf 2sg×2. The expression is found in the last stanza of the psalm and introduces p-vn-s n-s n n.

For Ps. *86* cf. above n. F 5. The expression is preceded by a section (vv. 9–10) devoid of formulaic language (cf. above E 1.3), and displaying motifs not otherwise found in the psalm. Exhortations asking for YHWH's support are found up to v. 6, v. 7 a describes the situation of invocation, and v. 7 b contains ki with impf 2sg, apparently expressing confidence. v. 11 opens with an imperative, which, as far as content is concerned, differs from the preceding exhortations and introduces modal impf 1sg (vv. 11 b–12). These modal impfa 1sg seem, however, to have different functions in context: v. 11 b is dependent upon the command of v. 11 a, while v. 12 a–b point to v. 13. vv. 12–13 show terminal traits (cf. F 4.2.5, G 5.2.4).

The following section, vv. 14–15, opens with references to a third party, not found in prior parts of the psalm; v. 15 lacks the initial ki of v. 5, 10, 13, vv. 16–17 seem to be the continuation of the previous section. Against this background I find it possible that vv. 12–13 form the conclusion of the first part of the psalm.

In Ps. *22*[56] the expression is preceded by a section (vv. 20–22 a) dominated by exhortations, leading up to perf 2sg-s1sg (v. 22 b).

In Pss. 61, 86 and 22 the expression is found at the outset of concluding sections. In Ps. 22, v. 23 is directly preceded by an account of divine intervention (perf 2sg); in Ps. 86, v. 12 contains two modal impfa 1sg followed by ki with a nominal and a verbal (perf 2sg) clause; Ps. 61 has two stanzas with modal impfa 1sg (v. 5, 9), the first of which precedes the perf 2sg (v. 6),

38

while the second seems to be dependent upon the modal impfa of vv. 7–8. Being closely associated with verbal clauses in the perfect, Ps. 86: 12 b and 22: 23 a have similar function in context—Ps. 61: 9 a, following upon modal impfa, is interpreted as conditional.

2.3.5. 59: 17 a–90: 14 a–92: 3 a–143: 8 a.

(V p-n+n-s)[57]

Of these four occurrences only Ps. *59* contains modal impf 1sg, but this psalm was not included in the starting group.

2.3.6. 138: 1 a–86: 12 a–9: 2 a–111: 1 a with 35: 18 a–43: 4 c–57: 10 a–18: 50 a– 71: 22 a.

(v N p-n+n-s with v-s p-N)[58]

Pss. *138, 9, 111, 35, 43*, and *57* did not form part of the starting group.

For Ps. *86* cf. above F 2.3.4.

In Ps. *18*[59] the expression is preceded by a section, initiated by participles (vv. 47–48 a), which lead into impf cons 3sg (v. 48 b), followed by another participle (v. 49 a) and two impfa 2sg-s1sg (v. 49 b–c). The impfa of v. 49 b–c must, in context, be interpreted in the present tense.

In Ps. *71* the expression is preceded by a section (vv. 19 b–20 b/21, cf. above n. F 38) with hymnic traits (v. 19 b–20 a), leading up to modal impfa (20 b–21).

In Pss. 86, 18 and 71 the expression is found in concluding sections. In Ps. 86, v. 12 is followed by motivations, the second of which contains perf 2sg with first person sing object; Ps. 18: 50 is introduced by ʿal ken, connecting the stanza with the preceding section, giving an account of divine intervention on behalf of the psalmist. Ps. 71: 22 is introduced by gam ʾani, which seems superfluous if the stanza is a direct continuation of v. 21—if, however, v. 22 is seen as the conclusion of vv. 2–5, 9–11 12–13 (cf. above n. F 38), v. 13 provides a background against which v. 22 a might be understood. If this interpretation is correct, the statement in Ps. 71: 22 a is conditional, while 86: 12 a and 18: 50 a are connected with direct accounts of divine intervention.

2.3.7. 35: 28–71: 24 a

(n-s, v n-s, n+n)[60]

Ps. *35* did not form part of the starting group, so there is no relevant comparative material to Ps. *71:* 24 a.

2.3.8. 52: 11 c–54: 8 b

(impf 1sg n-s part n)[61]

None of the psalms formed part of the starting group.

2.4. Cohortative-clauses in sing with instrumental qualifiers and YHWH as object (2 sing) are present in the following formulas and formulaic systems: 54:8–Jon. 2:10; 33:2–144:9. Under this heading I also include 92:5–143:5.

2.4.1. 54:8a–Jon. 2:10a

(p-N v p-s)[62]

Ps. 54 did not form part of the starting group, so there is no relevant comparative material to *Jon 2:* 10a.

2.4.2. 33:2b–144:9b

(p-n+n v p-s)[63]

None of the psalms formed part of the starting group.

2.4.3. 92:5b–143:5c

(p-n n-s v)[64]

Ps. 95 did not form part of the starting group, so there is no relevant comparative material to Ps. *143:* 5c.

2.5. Clauses in impf ind 1sg or cohortative sing with third person sing object are present in the following formulaic systems: 3:5–142:2a, 2b with related system in 77:2a, 2b; 13:6–Ex. 15:1; 104:33–146:2—cf. also 63:5; 7:18–9:3–92:2.

2.5.1. 3:5a–142:2a, 2b with 77:2a, 2b

(n-s p DN impf 1sg with n-s p DN x)[65]

Pss. 3 and 77 did not form part of the starting group so that there is no basis for comparison with Ps. *142:* 2.

2.5.2–4. None of the texts formed part of the starting group.

2.6. One formulaic system containing jussive is recorded in Culley's material: 88:3a–Jon. 2:8b–79:11a (v p-s N) with related system in 102:2b–18:7d (c-n-s p-s v)—cf. also 119:170a (v n-s p-s).[66]

Pss. 79 and *119* did not form part of the starting group.

In Ps. 88 the expression is found at the outset of the psalm. v. 2, 10b, and 14a contain perfa 1sg of *verba cordis* forming introductions to subsections (cf. above n. F 50). Parallel to the jussive is an imperative—these two are motivated in v. 4ff.

In *Jon.* 2 the expression is preceded within the stanza by a description of situation (p-vn) and perf 1sg, which governs the impf 3sg of v. 8b. If the interpretation of v. 8 as the counterpart of v. 3 is correct (cf. above n. F 15), Culley's classification "jussive" seems doubtful.

In Ps. *102* the expression is found at the outset of the psalm (vv. 2–4/12, cf. above n. F 30) and is preceded within the stanza by an exhortation; the imperative and the jussive, interpreted at the same level are, together with exhortations of v. 3, motivated in v. 4 ff.

In Ps. *18*, v. 7 is preceded by a description of misery (vv. 5–6), the terminology being similar to Jon. 2: 6–7 b. The stanza is initiated by a description of the invocational situation (vv. 7 a–b; impf 1sg of *verba cordis*), followed by impfa 3sg. The description of the relations between YHWH and the psalmist is taken up again in vv. 17–20 (cf. above n. F 59). vv. 8–16 lack first person sing objects, contain formulaic references to psalms outside the starting group, and show contents differing from those of the rest of the psalm—indications of a separate origin. Considering form and content, it is possible to regard vv. 7 and 17–20 as one section—a description of the invocational situation, leading into modal impfa (for v. 18–20 a cf. n. F 59), concluded by <u>ki</u> and perf 3sg; v. 7 d is thus to be interpreted as jussive, and forms the introduction to a section, dominated by modal impfa with motivations.

In Pss. 88 and 102 the expression is found at the outset of the units, in stanzas also containing clauses in the imperative; Ps. 18: 7 d too initiates a section—this, however, dominated by modal impfa 3sg. Thus 88: 3 a, 102: 2 b and 18: 7 d are found in sections displaying wishes concerning divine intervention, while Jon. 2: 8 b is governed by perf and refers back to statements of accomplished salvation.

3. Formulaic verbal clauses, comparing the psalmist with, or defining his relations to, a third party are present in three groups within Culley's material.

3.1. Verbal clauses in perf 1sg are found in 28: 1–143: 7–88: 5; 31: 14–Jr. 20: 10.

3.1.1. 28: 1 d–143: 7 d–88: 5 a

(v p n+n)[67]

For Ps. *28:* 1 cf. above 2.2.1.

In Ps. *143* the expression is immediately preceded by a negative command, and followed by further exhortations with motivations.

In Ps. *88* the expression is preceded by jussive–imperative (v. 3, cf. above 2.6), motivated by <u>ki</u> and perf (v. 4). vv. 5–8 seem to be an exposition of this motivation (cf. שאול in v.4 b—בור in 5 a, 7 a—מתים in 6 a—קבר in 6 b—מצלות in 7 b—משבריך in 8 b).

vv. 9–10 a contain further descriptions of misery.

28: 1 d and 143: 7 d are seen as having similar function in context; the expressions depict the negative consequences[68] which would follow if YHWH would fail to comply with the preceding exhortation, while 88: 5 a forms part of a rather detailed description of misery, and does not immediately follow an exhortation.

3.1.2. 31: 14 a–b–Jr. 20: 10 a–b
(part v n+n n p-n)[69]

*Jr. 20* did not form part of the starting group, so there is no basis for comparison with Ps. *31:* 14 a–b.

3.2. One verbal clause in impf 1sg is present in the material:
118: 6–56: 5–56: 12.
(x neg v inter v p-s n)[70]

Ps. *118* did not form part of the starting group, so there is no basis for comparison with Ps. *56:* 5, *56:* 12.

4. Systematization and contextual remarks.

4.1. Realizations of set phrases from psalms within the starting group, found in formulas or formulaic systems otherwise composed of material not included in that group, articulate thoughts and motifs of little relevance for this investigation. This is also true, according to my premises, of realizations of formulas and formulaic systems for which no common function in context can be isolated; set phrases differing from the other members of a formula/system concerning function in context might give structural indications.

4.1.1. Set phrases found in formulas or formulaic systems otherwise composed of material not belonging to the starting group: 26: 6 a, 7 b, 30: 7 b, 31: 8 a, 14 a–b, 56: 5, 12, 71: 24 a, 102: 3 b, 109: 22 b, 142: 2 a, 2 b, 7 b, 143: 5 a, 5 b, 5 c, 8 a, Jon. 2: 3 a–b, 10 a.

4.1.2. Formulas and formulaic systems without similar function in context: 86: 1 c–109: 22 a–25 16 c (for 40: 18 a–69: 30 a cf. F 1.1.1), 116: 16 b–143: 12 c, 142: 4 a–Jon. 2: 8 a (for 143: 4 a cf. F 4.1.4), 31: 10 b–(Lm. 1: 20–) 69: 18 b, 6: 8–31: 10 c, (32: 8 a–) 142: 4 c, 143: 8 c, 56: 5 b–c–56: 12 1–b– 26: 1 c–d, 142: 6 a–30: 3 b with 88: 14 a (for 30: 9 a–Jo. 1: 19 a–28: 1 a with 61: 3 a–86: 3 b cf. F 2.2.1.)

4.1.3. Set phrases with differing functions within formulas and formulaic systems: 25: 1, 2 a, 20 d, 61: 9 a, 71: 22 a, 86: 3 b, 88: 5 a, 140: 7 a, 143: 8 d, Is. 38: 10 a, Jo. 1: 19, Jon. 2: 8 b.

4.1.4. For 143: 4 a cf. above n. F 13, for 26: 3 b–86: 11 b cf. F 2.1.6.

4.2.1. Formulaic nominal clauses pertaining to the psalmist contain descriptions of quality or state. The set phrases initiated by <u>ki</u> motivate exhortations of various kinds (86: 1 c, 109: 22 a, 25: 16 c, 143: 12 c, 31: 10 b and 69: 18 b, note the exception 116: 16 b)—and lead in Ps. 109: 22 and 31: 10 into rather extensive, non-formulaic descriptions of misery (mainly in the perf). The clauses initiated by <u>waw</u> delimit and emphasize the qualities of the psalmist as compared with a third party, and lead up to modal impfa in concluding parts (40: 18 a, 69: 30 a). The prepositional phrases of Ps. 142: 4 a and Jon. 2: 8 a are found within descriptions of misery—in the first case preceded by impfa 1sg, in the second followed by perf 1sg and impfcons.

Similar function in context was isolated only for 40: 18 a–69: 30 a.

4.2.2. Formulaic verbal clauses in perf 1sg are found in summarizing or transitional sections expressing confidence, and in reviews containing *verba cordis:* in Ps. 31: 2 a–b, 71: 1 a–b and 26: 1 c–d as headings; in Ps. 30: 7 a, Jon. 2: 5 a, 31: 15 a, 31: 23 a and 116: 11 a preceded by statements concerning accomplished salvation, and describing the reactions of the psalmist in a former situation of misery. The exhortations of Ps. 6: (2-)5, 31: 10 a and 102: 2–3 are followed by motivating <u>ki</u>-clauses, introducing rather detailed descriptions of misery (mainly in the perf). Ps. 102: 4 a and 31: 10 c–11 a are found at the outsets of such descriptions, Ps. 6: 8 a in the conclusion. Ps. 143: 8 b, 28: 1 d and 143: 7 d are found as motivations to exhortations, while Ps. 142: 6 forms the transition between a description of need and a section containing exhortations and motivations.

Ps. 25: 2, 25: 20 d, 30: 3, 56: 5, 56: 12, 140: 7 and Is. 38: 10 do not fit into any of the above categories.

Similar functions in context were isolated for Ps. 30: 7 a–Jon. 2: 5 a, 31: 23 a–116: 11 a, 31: 11 a–102: 4 a, 31: 2 a–b – 71: 1 a–b and 31: 15 b–142: 6 b.

4.2.3. Formulaic verbal clauses in impf ind 1sg describe the invocational activity (30: 9 a, 28: 1 a, 61: 3 a) in opening sections and are interpreted as iterative, 88: 14 a contains *perf 1sg,* also describing invocational activity.

The iterative impfa 1sg of Ps. 142: 4 c (latter part) and 143: 8 c (outset) qualify preceding or following verbal clauses, those of Ps. 86: 3 b, 4 b constitute motivations for preceding exhortations. Similar function in context was isolated for Ps. 30: 9 a–28: 1 a–61: 3 a.

4.2.4. Modal impfa 2/3sg are found at the outset of sections, containing exhortations dealing with divine intervention (88: 3 a, 102: 2 b and 18: 7 d)— Ps. 88: 3 a and 102: 2 b are parallel to clauses in the imperative.

4.2.5. Modal impfa 1sg were found in concluding sections [18: 50 a, (22: 23 a), 61: 9 a, 71: 22 a, (86: 12 a) 12 b].

Similar functions in context were isolated for Ps. 86: 12 b–22: 23 a, 86: 12 b–18: 50 a.


G. 1. Nominal clauses pertaining to YHWH; verbal clauses in the perf or impf with YHWH as subject, and lacking direct object.

1.1. Of 17 registered groups of nominal formulaic clauses[1] only three contain references to two or more psalms from the starting group: 31: 5–71: 5–91: 9–143: 10–43: 2–25: 5 with possible variant in 22: 10; 71: 3–31: 4–40: 18–119: 114; 63: 4–109: 21 with 69: 17. References to material from the starting group are also found in 35: 10–71: 19–89: 9 (Culley no. 39); 103: 8–Jo. 2: 13–86: 15 (no. 55); 18: 35–144: 1 (no. 122); 18: 31–Pr. 30: 5 (no. 169).

1.1.1. 31: 5 b–71: 5 a–91: 9 a–143: 10 b–43: 2 a–25: 5 c; 22: 10 a
(part pr N-s)[2]
Pss. 91 and 43 did not form part of the starting group.
In Ps. 31 the expression is found in the opening section (vv. 2 c–5, cf. above n. F 17). Formulaic language is present in v. 2 a–b, 2 c, 3 a, 4 a, 5 a and 5 b. The four commands of vv. 2 c–3 are followed by a motivating nominal ki-clause, expressing confidence (v. 4 a), and three modal impfa 2sg-s1sg (v. 4 b–5 a); the motivation is given in the nominal clause of v. 5 b. A reference to the activities of a third party is found in v. 5 aβ (perf 3pl).
In Ps. 71 the expression is found in the opening section (vv. 2–5, cf. above n. F 38). Formulaic language is present in v. 2 a, 2 c, 3 d, 4 a and 5 a. vv. 2–3 contain general exhortations (modal impfa and impv), v. 4 specifies the situation referring to a third party; the motivations are given in the nominal clauses of v. 5 a and 5 b.
In Ps. 143 two sections are characterized by exhortations with motivations (vv. 1–4 and 7–10 b, cf. above n. F 12)—the expression forms the concluding motivation within the second of these. Formulaic language is present in v. 7 a, 7 c, 7 d, 8 a, 8 b, 8 c, 8 d, 9 a, and 10 b. The exhortations contain various injunctions, the motivations in v. 8 b, 8 d, 9 a and 10 b deal with the relation between YHWH and the psalmist. v. 9 a contains a reference to a third party.
In Ps. 25 the expression forms a motivation within the section 4–7 (cf. above n. F 6). Formulaic language is present in v. 5 c. The four exhortations of vv. 4–5 b belong to an "instruction" category (cf. above n. F 12 on Ps. 143: 8 c, 10 a) and derive their motivation from the relation between YHWH and the psalmist (v. 5 b–c); vv. 6–7 have זכר ×3 with references to YHWH's attributes.
In Ps. 22 the expression is found at the outset of the psalm, within the sub-

44

section 7–11 (cf. above n. F 56). Formulaic language is found in v. 9 c and 10 a. vv. 7–9 contain an exposition of the activities of a hostile third party, v. 10 picks up the (scornful) quotation from v. 9, transforming it, through a confirmative ki, into a statement of confidence.

In Pss. 31 and 71 the expressions are immediately preceded by exhortations containing references to a third party—the nominal clauses initiated with ki motivate these exhortations. Both contexts are characterized by a relatively large proportion of formulaic language.

In Pss. 143 and 25 the expressions are directly preceded by exhortations, expressing wishes for divine guidance—the nominal clauses initiated with ki motivate these exhortations. The context of 143: 10 b shows, when compared to that of 25: 5 c, a greater variation as far as the content of the commands is concerned, and displays nine instances of formulaic language against one in Ps. 25. Ps. 22: 10 a does not form a motivation but rather expounds the preceding stanza.

### 1.1.2.  71: 3 d–31: 4 a–40: 18 c–119: 114 a

(n-s c-n-s pr)[3]

Ps. *119* did not form part of the starting group.

For Ps. *71* and *31* cf. above G 1.1.1.

For Ps. *40:* 18 cf. above F 1.1.1. The concluding stanza is introduced by a contrasting nominal clause, forming the background to the following modal impf 2sg (v. 18 a–b); the latter part of the stanza contains another nominal clause, forming the background to the following negative command (v. 18 c–d).

Ps. 71: 3 d and 31: 4 a are both found in opening, formulaic sections and provide motivations for one of several exhortations, mainly dealing with "listening" and "saving", while Ps. 40 shows a different structure within the section.

### 1.1.3.  63: 4 a–109: 21 b (-c); 69: 17 (a-) b.

(part adj n-s x)[4]

Ps. *63* did not form part of the starting group.

For Ps. *69:* 17 cf. above F 1.2.2. The expression is the motivation for the first of six exhortations within the section.

In Ps. *109* the expression is found in a section (vv. 21–25, 26–27, cf. above n. F 5) introduced by an exhortation and a motivating nominal ki-clause (v. 21 a–b). The following exhortation (v. 21 c) is motivated in the same way, but here the ki-clause (v. 22 a) introduces a rather detailed description of personal misery (vv. 22 b–25, with the exception of v. 25 b–c in the perfect). Formulaic language is present in v. 21 b–c, 22 a, 22 b, 26 b.

109: 21 b (-c) and 69: 17 (a-) b are both found at the outset of sections containing exhortations and motivations; in 69: 17–20 these are evenly distributed throughout the section, in 109: 21–25 the exhortations are found at the outset, and the second motivation is expanded into a lengthy description—109: 21 b (-c) and 69: 17 (a-) b are thus found in different types of contexts.

1.2. 13 formulaic verbal clauses which have YHWH as subject, but which do not define His relations to the psalmist or to a third party, are present in Culley's material.[5] Of these, the groups 67, 134, 172 and 174 contain references to material from the starting group (18: 9–50: 3–97: 3; 18: 11–104: 3; 18: 10–144: 5; 18: 15–144: 6), but only to one psalm. Under this heading I also include the system 102: 13–Lm. 5: 19 (pr DN p-n v n-s p-n c-n).[6]

2. Formulaic verbal clauses defining the relation between YHWH (second or third person) and the psalmist.

2.1. Verbal clauses in perf 2sg with first person sing object are present in the following formulaic systems: 69: 20–142: 4–139: 2–Jr. 17: 16, and 69: 6; 59: 17–61: 4–63: 8–Is. 25: 4; 56: 14–116: 8–86: 13. Perfa 3sg with first person sing objects are found in 13: 6–142: 8–116: 7.

2.1.1. 69: 20 a–142: 4 b–139: 2 a–Jr. 17: 16 c, 69: 6 a.
(pr v N-s)[7]

Ps. *139* and *Jr. 17* did not form part of the starting group.

For Ps. *69:* 20 cf. F 1.2.2. The expression is found in the concluding stanza of the section. The exhortations are motivated by references to YHWH's attributes (v. 17 b, 17 c), to the state of the psalmist (v. 18 b), and to a third party (v. 19 b); v. 20 seems to be the principal motivation for the preceding exhortations (cf. Ps. 86: 5, also initiated by a personal pronoun).

For Ps. *142:* 4 cf. F 1.2.1. vv. 2–4 b describe the invocation, vv. 4 c–5 account for a situation of need, v. 6 for the actions of the psalmist in this situation (*verba cordis* in the perfect), and vv. 7–8 cite his exhortations. v. 4 b is the only expression of confidence in the unit, following directly upon a statement of uncertainty.

In Ps. *69*, v. 6 concludes the opening section (vv. 2–6, cf. above n. F 7). Formulaic language is present in v. 2 b, 5 a, 5 b and 6. The initiating exhortation is motivated by descriptions of the situation and activities of the psalmist (vv. 2 b–5 in the perf). v. 6 picks up אלהים from v. 2 a, which, together with the personal pronoun, stresses v. 6 as the principal motivation for the initial exhortation.

Ps. 69: 20 a and 69: 6 a could be ascribed similar function in context—two realizations of the same system within one unit do not, however, provide criteria for isolating set phrases common to a group of psalms.

2.1.2.   59: 17 c–61: 4 a–63: 8 a–Is. 25: 4 a.
(part v n p-N)[8]
Pss. *59, 63* and *Is. 25* did not form part of the starting group and thus there is no relevant comparative material to Ps. *61: 4* a.

2.1.3.   56: 14 a–116: 8 a–86: 13 b.
(perf 2sg n-s p-N)[9]
In Ps. *56* the expression is found in the concluding section (vv. 13–14, cf. above n. F 45) and provides the motivation for the modal impf 1sg-clause of v. 13. The latter part of v. 14 reports the consequences of YHWH's intervention (cf. also Ps. 116: 9).

In Ps. *116* the expression is found in the first part of the psalm within the subsection 7–8 (cf. above n. F 9), forming the second of two motivations (v. 7 b, 8 a) to an exhortation expressing confidence. v. 9 (cf. also 56: 14) concludes the first part of the psalm.

For Ps. *86: 13* cf. F 2.3.4.

56: 14 a, 116: 8 a and 86: 13 b are found in concluding sections, and are closely connected with vows (56: 13, 86: 12) and/or expressions of confidence (116: 7 a, 86: 11 b, 13 a, 56: 14 c). The expressions are seen as having similar function in context.

2.1.4.   13: 6 d–142: 8 d–116: 7 b.
(part v p-s)[10]
Ps. *13* did not form part of the starting group.
In Ps. *142* the expression concludes the psalm. The section 7–8 (cf. above n. F 14) contains three exhortations (v. 7 a, 7 d, 8 a), in v. 7 b and 7 d motivated by ki and perf, in v. 8 introducing a statement of consequence—this, in turn, followed by modal impf 3sg and ki with impf 2sg. Formulaic language is present in v. 7 a, 7 b, 7 c, 8 a, and 8 d.

For Ps. *116: 7* cf. G 2.1.3.

142: 8 d and 116: 7 d are found in concluding sections and are preceded by exhortations. These exhortations, however, differ in content: Ps. 142: 7–8 contain summons to "listen" and "save", 116: 7 a expresses confidence. In Ps. 116, v. 7 b and 8 a (ki with perf 3/2sg) are seen as referring to accomplished salvation, while Ps. 142 does not contain such references—the impf 2sg must therefore be interpreted as modal.

No set correlation could be established between phrase and context.

2.2. Verbal clauses in impf 3sg with first person sing object are present in the following formulaic systems: 18: 48–47: 4–144: 2; 18: 19–94: 22 with 9: 10, 18: 20–22: 9. Under this heading I also include 38: 3–32: 4; 118: 14–Ex. 15: 2– Is. 12: 2. Impfa 2sg with first person sing objects are found in 18: 49– 140: 2, 5; 128: 5–134: 3; 31: 21–61: 5 with 17: 8–36: 8–57: 2–63: 8.

2.2.1–2. 18: 48 b–47: 4 a–144: 2 b and 18: 19 b–94: 22 a, 9: 10 a
(x N p-s)[11] and (c-v DN p-n p-s, c-v DN n p-N)[12]

Pss. *47*, *144*, *94* and *9* did not form part of the starting group and thus there is no relevant comparative material to Ps. *18:* 48 b and *18:* 19 b.

2.2.3. 18: 20 b–c – 22: 9 c–d
(impf 3 sg-s part v p-s)[13]

In Ps. *18* the expression forms the conclusion of the section 7+17–20 (cf. above n. F 59), dominated by clauses in the impf (v. 7 c, 7 d, 17 a, 17 b, 17 c, 18 a, 19 a, 20 b; impf cons in 19 b, 20 a) motivated by <u>ki</u> and perf in 18 b and 20 b. The impfa are interpreted as modal. Formulaic language is present in 7 d, 18 a, 18 b, 19 b and 20 b–c.

In Ps. *22* the expression is found at the outset, in a sub-section (vv. 7–11, cf. above n. F 56 and G 1.1.1) displaying an exposition of the activities of a third party. v. 9 is seen as a quotation, followed by statements of confidence.

The expressions do not have similar function in context.

2.2.4–5. 38: 3 b–32: 4 b and 118: 14–Ex. 15: 2 a–b – Is. 12: 2 c–d.
(v p-s n-s)[14] and (n-s c-n DN c-v p-s p-n)[15]

None of the texts formed part of the starting group.

2.2.6. 18: 49 c–140: 2 b, 5 b.
(p-n+n impf 2sg-s)[16]

For Ps. *18* cf. above F 2.3.6.

In Ps. *140* the expression is found in the opening section (vv. 2–4, cf. above n. F 40). v. 2 a contains an exhortation, v. 2 b impf 2sg-s1sg—the cola show similar contents and the impf of v. 2 b must be interpreted at the same level as the impv of v. 2 a. The section 5–6 is similar in structure, and the impf of v. 5 b is interpreted at the same level as the impv of v. 5 a.

18: 49 and 140: 2, 5 seem to have different functions in context in that the expression in Ps. 18 refers back to earlier sections (vv. 31/32–46) and forms part of a hymnic section, while the interpretation of Ps. 140: 2 and 5 is determined by the preceding impv.

2.2.7. 128: 5 a–134: 3 a.
(v-s DN p-n)[17]

None of the psalms formed part of the starting group.

2.2.8. 31: 21 a–61: 5 b with 17: 8 b–36: 8 b–57: 2 c–63: 8 b.
(v p-n+n-s with p-n+n-s v)[18]

Pss. *36, 57* and *63* did not form part of the starting group. Ps. *31:* 21 a shows impf 2sg-s*3plur*, Ps. *61:* 5 b cohortative sing—these two will not be analyzed under this heading, so that there remains no relevant comparative material to Ps. *17:* 8 b (cf. G 4).

3. Clauses in the imperative,[19] dealing with the relation YHWH—the psalmist, are present in the following formulas and formulaic systems: 31: 3–71: 2–102: 3 with related system in 88: 3–17: 6, and, in the perfect, 116: 2—cf. also 86: 1; 54: 4–143: 1–102: 2–84: 9 with variation in 39: 13; 55: 2–86: 6–61: 2, and, in the perfect, 6: 10; 17: 1 b–17: 1 c–17: 6–61: 2; 27: 7–64: 2–141: 1; 86: 6–140: 7–28: 2, and, in the perfect, 66: 19–31: 23 with 6: 9–28: 6; 25: 16–86: 16–119: 132; 31: 17–109: 26–6: 5; 27: 11–86: 11–119: 33; 142: 7–143: 9–59: 2–31: 16, and, in the imperfect 18: 18; 9: 14–25: 18–119: 153; 6: 3–31: 10–56: 2–86: 3 with related system in 6: 3–26: 1–69: 17; 25: 20–86: 2–17: 13–120: 2 with 6: 5–116: 4; 31: 2–119: 40 with variant in the imperfect in 71: 2, and possibly related 143: 1–54: 3; 40: 14–71: 12–22: 20 with 38: 23; 69: 18–102: 3 with 143: 7; 27: 9–102: 3–143: 7 with variation in 69: 18, and, as interjection, 13: 2–88: 15—cf. also 22: 25 in the perfect; 35: 22–38: 22–71: 12, and, in a shorter form, 22: 12, with variation in 28: 1, and possible variation in 22: 20; 35: 22–39: 13–109: 1 with 83: 2; 142: 7–143: 1 with 54: 4; 5: 9–27: 11; 22: 21–142: 8 with variation in the imperfect in 143: 11; 71: 4–140: 5; 51: 3–119: 58; 57: 2–123: 3; 6: 2–38: 2; 27: 12–41: 3; 6: 5–90: 13; Lm. 1: 11–Lm. 2: 20; 80: 15–142: 5– Is. 63: 15; 38: 22–27: 9 with 119: 8 and 71: 9–71: 18.

3.1. 31: 3 a–71: 2 c–102: 3 c with 88: 3 b–17: 6 c, 116: 2 a, and 86: 1 a–b.
(impv p-s n-s with impv n-s p-N, perf n-s p-N, impv n-s x)[20]

In Ps. *31* the expression is found in the section 2 c–5 (cf. above n. F 17 and G 1.1.1).

In Ps. *71* the expression is found in the section 2–5 (cf. above n. F 38 and G 1.1.1).

In Ps. *102* the expression is found at the outset (vv. 2–4/12, cf. above n. F 30). v. 2 a, 2 b, 3 a, 3 c and 3 d contain exhortations; the motivations of v. 4 ff. account for the miserable condition of the psalmist. Formulaic language is present in v. 2 a, 2 b, 3 a, 3 b, 3 c, 3 d and 4 a.

In Ps. *88* the related expression is found in the section 3–4/10 a (cf. above n. F 50). v. 3 a and 3 b contain exhortations, which are motivated in v. 4 ff.

by an account of the miserable condition of the psalmist. Formulaic language is present in v. 3 a, 3 b and 5 a.

In Ps. *17* the expression is found at the outset of the section 6 c–9/12.[21] v. 6 c, 6 d, 7 a, 8 a and 8 b contain exhortations; the latter part of v. 7 and v. 9 refer to a hostile third party. Formulaic language is present in v. 6 c, 6 d and 8 b.

The perfect clause of Ps. *116:* 2 a is the only example of formulaic language within a section (vv. 1–2, cf. above n. F 9), forming the summarizing heading of the psalm. The expression constitutes the second of two motivations for the initial perf 1sg.

In Ps. *86* the expression is found at the outset (vv. 1–5, cf. above n. F 3). v. 1 a, 1 b, 2 a, 2 c, 3 a and 4 a contain exhortations, in v. 1 c and 2 b motivated by <u>ki</u> and nominal clauses, in v. 3 b and 4 b by impfa 1sg. v. 5 constitutes the motivation for the whole section. Formulaic language is present in v. 1 a, 1 b, 1 c, 2 a, 2 b, 3 a, 3 b and 4 b.

With the exception of 116: 2 a all the expressions are found at the outset of sections displaying exhortations with motivations. 31: 3 a, 71: 2 c, 102: 3 c, 17: 6 c and 86: 1 a are followed by further commands within the stanza, 88: 3 b is preceded by modal impf—these six are seen as having similar function in context.

## 3.2. 54: 4 a–143: 1 a–102: 2 a–84: 9 with 39: 13 a.

(DN impv n-s with impv n-s DN)[22]

Pss. *54, 84* and *139* did not form part of the starting group.

In Ps. *143* the expression is found at the outset (vv. 1–4, cf. above n. F 12). The exhortations are concentrated to vv. 1–2 a, and motivated by references to general unrighteousness (v. 2 b) and the activities of a hostile third party (v. 3, in the perf); v. 4 describes the personal state of the psalmist (in the impf). Formulaic language is present in v. 1 a, 1 b, 1 c, 3 a, 3 b, 3 c and 4 a.

For Ps. *102:* 2 cf. above G 3.1.

Both expressions are found at the outset of the psalms, in sections characterized by exhortations and motivations—143: 1 a and 102: 2 a have similar function in context.

## 3.3. 55: 2 a–86: 6 a–61: 2 a, and 6: 10 a.

(impv DN n-s and perf DN n-s)[23]

Ps. *55* did not form part of the starting group.

Ps. *86* is structured by the expressions of confidence in v. 5, 8, 10, 13, 15 and 17 c (cf. above n. F 3). v. 6 is thus found at the outset of the second section (vv. 6–8); the exhortations of v. 6 a and 6 b are not explicitly motivated but followed by a description of situation (v. 7 a), and k̲i̲ with impf 2sg-s1sg (v. 7 b). Formulaic language is present in v. 6 a and 6 b.

In Ps. *61* the double exhortation of v. 2 is followed by a description of situation (cf. above F 2.2.1). Formulaic language is present in v. 2 a, 2 b and 3 a.

The variant expression in Ps. *6:* 10 a is found in the concluding section (vv. 9–11, cf. above n. F 26), forms the second of two motivations (v. 9 b, 10 a) for the initial exhortation, and introduces modal impf 3sg (v. 10 b–11). Formulaic language is present in v. 9 b, 10 a and 11 a.

86: 6 a and 61: 2 a are found at the outset of sections, followed, within the stanzas, by other exhortations, and further by descriptions of situation, introducing modal impf 2/3sg. The expressions have similar function in context; for clauses in perf 2/3sg cf. G 2.1.

3.4.  17: 1 b–17: 1 c–17: 6 d–61: 2 a
(impv n-s)[24]

In Ps. *17* v. 1 b and 1 c are followed by modal impfa (v. 2), while vv. 3–5 contain statements of blamelessness (cf. above n. G 21). Formulaic language is present in v. 1 b and 1 c.

For Ps. *17:* 6 cf. G 3.1.

For Ps. *61:* 2 cf. G 3.3.

No set correlation could be established between phrase and context.

3.5.  27: 7 a–b – 64: 2 a–141: 1 c.
(impv n-s x)[25]

None of the psalms formed part of the starting group.

3.6.  86: 6 b–140: 7 b–28: 2 a and 66: 19 b–31: 23 c with 6: 9 b–28: 6 b.
(impv n+n-s and perf n+n-s with part perf n+n-s).[26]

Ps. *66* did not form part of the starting group.

For Ps. *86:* 6 cf. G 3.3.

In Ps. *140* the expression is found in a section (vv. 7–8, cf. above n. F 40) dominated by statements of confidence. v. 7 opens with an "'āmarti"-phrase, followed by the exhortation. As perf 1sg אמר has been found to introduce reviews, (cf. F 1.3.1.1, 2.1.2) v. 7 b is seen as a quotation. Formulaic language is present in v. 7 a and 7 b.

In Ps. *28* the expression is found in the opening section (vv. 1–2, cf. above n. F 48). v. 1 a outlines the situation and is followed by a negative command (v. 1 b) and statements of consequence (v. 1 c–d); v. 2 contains an exhortation and another description of situation. Formulaic language is present in v. 1 a, 1 b, 1 d and 2 a.

In Ps. *31* the expression is found in a concluding section (vv. 22–23; cf. above n. F 17 and F 1.3.1.1). For Ps. *6:* 9 cf. G 3.3.

In Ps. *28:* 6 the expression forms part of a section (vv. 6–7, cf. above n. F 48) with terminal traits, and constitutes the motivation for the preceding "bārūk"-statement. v. 6 b is the only example of formulaic language within the section.

In Ps. 86 and 28[I] the expression is found at the outset of sections, and is followed by descriptions of situation; 140: 7 b, preceded by an "'āmarti"-phrase, is considered a quotation. 86: 6 b and 28: 2 a have similar function in context—from this differs 140: 7 b.

The perfect clauses in Ps. 31: 23 c, 6: 9 b and 28: 6 b are all found in concluding sections.

3.7. 25: 16 a–b – 86: 16 a–b – 119: 132 a–b

(impv p-s c-impv-s)[27]

Ps. *119* did not form part of the starting group.

For Ps. *25:* 16 cf. F 1.1.1.

In Ps. *86* the expression is found at the outset of the conclusion (vv. 16–17, cf. above n. F 3). v. 16 a–b constitute the first of five exhortations (vv. 16–17 a), followed by modal impfa 3pl and ki with perfa 2sg. No other example of formulaic language is found within the section.

Ps. 25: 16 a–b and 86: 16 a–b have similar function in context.

3.8. 31: 17 b–109: 26 b–6: 5 c.

(impv-s p-n-s)[28]

For Ps. *31:* 17 cf. F 2.1.2.

For Ps. *109:* 26 cf. above n. F 5, F 1.1.1.

In Ps. *6* the expression is found in the opening section (vv. 2–6, cf. above n. F 26). v. 2 a, 2 b, 3 a, 3 c, 5 a, 5 b and 5 c contain exhortations; motivations in the form of ki-clauses are found in v. 3 b and 3 d, while v. 5 b has l[e]ma'an. v. 6 is not immediately preceded by an exhortation and is seen as a general motivation for the whole section. Formulaic language is present in v. 2 a, 2 b, 3 a, 3 b, 3 c, 3 d, 5 a, 5 b and 5 c.

109: 26 b and 6: 5 c are found in sections, characterized by exhortations and motivations—the latter mainly in the form of ki-clauses (109: 21 c, 22 a, 6: 3 b, 3 d), and descriptions of personal misery (109: 22 b–25, 6: 4 a). 109: 26 b introduces statements of consequence, 6: 5 c a ki-clause with general contents—the two expressions are nevertheless seen as having similar function in context. Ps. 31: 17 b is regarded as a quotation.

3.9. 27: 11 a–86: 11 a–119: 33 a.

(impv-s DN N-s)[29]

Pss. *27* and *119* did not form part of the starting group and thus there is no relevant comparative material to Ps. *86:* 11 a.

3.10.  142: 7 c–d–143: 9 a–59: 2 a–31: 16 b and 18: 18 (a).
(impv-s p-N-s and impf-s p-n-s)[30]
Ps. *59* did not form part of the starting group.
For Ps. *142:* 7 cf. G 2.1.4.
For Ps. *143:* 9 a cf. G 1.1.1.
For Ps. *31:* 16 b cf. G 3.8 and F 2.1.2.
For Ps. 18: 18 a cf. G 2.2.3.
Ps. 142: 7 c, 143: 9 a, and 18: 18 a are found in contexts dominated by exhortations with motivations, while Ps. 31: 15–17/18 b constitutes a review—the exhortation in v. 16 b is a quotation.

3.11.  9: 14 b–25: 18 a–119: 153 a–b.
(impv n-s x)[31]
Pss. *9* and *119* did not form part of the starting group, and thus there is no relevant comparative material to Ps. *25:* 18 a.

3.12. 6: 3 a–b–31: 10 a–b–56: 2 a–b–86: 3 with 6: 3 c–d–26: 1 a–b–69: 17 a–b.
(impv-s DN part x with impv-s DN part x)[32]
For Ps. *6:* 3 cf. G 3.8.
For Ps. *31:* 10 cf. F 1.2.2.
In Ps. *56* the expression is found in the opening section (vv. 2–3/4, cf. above n. F 45) and represents the only exhortation and the sole example of formulaic language within that section. The motivation (v. 2 b) refers to a third party, who is described in vv. 2 c–3. v. 4 is unintelligible.
For Ps. *86:* 3 cf. G 3.1.
For Ps. *26:* 1 cf. n. F 46.
For Ps. *69:* 17 cf. F 1.2.2. The expression constitutes the first of six exhortations within the section.
Ps. 31: 10 a(–b) and 56: 2 a(–b) are the only exhortations within their sections and introduce motivating ki-clauses, which are developed in the following stanzas in non-formulaic language. The expressions have similar function in context.
6: 3 a(–b), c(–d)–86: 3 a(–b) and 69: 17 a(–b) are found in sections, characterized by exhortations and motivations which are evenly distributed. The expressions have similar function in context.
Ps. 26: 1 a(–b) does not belong to any of these categories.

3.13. 25: 20 a–b–86: 2 a–b–17: 13 d–120: 2 a with 6: 5 a–b–116: 4 b–c.
(impv n-s x with x impv n-s)[33]

Ps. *120* did not form part of the starting group.

For Ps. *25:* 20 cf. G 3.7. and F 1.1.1.

For Ps. *86:* 2 cf. G 3.1.

In Ps. *17:* 13 the expression is found in a section (vv. 13–14, cf. above n. G 21) containing four exhortations, followed by min and a description of a third party. v. 17 d is the only example of formulaic language within the section.

For Ps. *6:* 5 cf. G 3.8.

For Ps. *116:* 4 cf. above n. F 9 and 10.

Ps. 25: 20 a(–b), 86: 2 a(–b) and 6: 5 (a–) b are all found in contexts with evenly distributed commands and motivations; if 116: 3–9 is seen as a "telescoped lament" (cf. n. F 9), 116: 4 (b–) c could be added to the above three, forming a group of expressions with similar function in context.

In Ps. 17 the context is obscure, but the expression here seems to introduce a description; furthermore, no other examples of formulaic language are found within the section.

3.14. 31: 2 c–119: 40 b with 71: 2 a and possibly 143: 1 c–54: 3 a.

(p-n-s impv-s with p-n-s impf-s and p-n-s impv-s)[34]

Pss. *119* and *54* did not form part of the starting group.

For Ps. *31:* 2 and *71:* 2 cf. G 1.1.1.

For Ps. *143:* 1 cf. G 3.2.

The three expressions are found at the outset of opening sections, and are followed by further exhortations with motivations.

Ps. 31: 2 c, 71: 2 a and 143: 1 c have similar function in context.

3.15. 40: 14 b–71: 12 b–22: 20 b with 38: 23 b.

(DN p-n-s impv with impv p-n-s DN)[35]

Ps. *38* did not form part of the starting group.

In Ps. *40* the expression is found in the section 14–18 (cf. F 1.1.1.). The exhortations of v. 14 a and 14 b are followed by wishes (modal impfa) concerning a third party—negative in vv. 15–16, positive in v. 17. In v. 18 nominal clauses (v. 18 a, 18 c) precede modal impfa.

In Ps. *71* the expression is found in the section 12–13 (cf. above n. F 38), initiated by two exhortations, which are followed by wishes (modal impfa) concerning a third party.

Formulaic language is present in v. 12 a, 12 b, 13 a and 13 b.

In Ps. *22* the expression is found in the section 20–22 a/b (cf. above n. F 56) displaying four exhortations (v. 20 a, 20 b, 21 a, 22 a) with references to a third party, here in the guise of different animals. Formulaic language is present in v. 20 a, 20 b, 21 a.

In Pss. 40, 71 and 22 the expressions are preceded by other exhortations with similar contents. Ps. 40: 14 b and 71: 12 b are followed by wishes concerning a third party, while Ps. 22: 22 b contains perf 2sg–s1sg; as both modal impfa 3pl and perf 2/3sg are found as conclusions of psalms within the starting group (cf. G 5.2.4) Ps. 40: 14 b, 71: 12 b and 22: 20 b are seen as having similar function in context.

3.16. 69: 18 b–c – 102: 3 e with 143: 7 a.
(x impv impv-s with impv impv-s x)[36]
For Ps. *69:* 18 cf. F 1.2.2.
For Ps. *102:* 3 cf. G 3.1.
For Ps. *143:* 7 cf. F 1.3.2.4.
The expressions have similar function in context.

3.17. 27: 9 a–102: 3 a–143: 7 c with 69: 18 a and 13: 2 b–88: 15, and 22: 25 c.
(neg v n-s p-s with neg v n-s p-N and inter v n-s p-s and neg v n-s p-s)[37]
Pss. *27* and *13* did not form part of the starting group.
For Ps. *102:* 3, *143:* 7 and *69:* 18 cf. G 3.16.
The interjections are of minor interest under this heading; the perfect clause of Ps. 22: 25 is the only example of formulaic language in vv. 24–32, and the context lacks exhortations.

3.18. 35: 22 c–38: 22 b–71: 12 a and 22: 12 a with 28: 1 b and possibly 22: 20 a
(DN neg v p-s and neg v p-s with neg v n-s and DN neg v)[38]
Pss. *35* and *38* did not form part of the starting group.
For Ps. *71:* 12 and *22:* 20 cf. G 3.15.
The "shorter form" in Ps. *22:* 12 is found at the outset of a section (vv. 12–17/19, cf. above n. F 56) and introduces a lengthy description of personal misery.
For Ps. *28* cf. G 3.6.
71: 12 a and 22: 20 a show similar function in context (cf. also G 3.15), from this differ both 22: 12 a and 28: 1 b.

3.19. 35: 22 a–b – 39: 13 c–109: 1 with 83: 2 b
(x neg v with neg v x)[39]
Pss. *35, 39* and *83* did not form part of the starting group and thus there is no basis for comparison with Ps. *109:* 1.

3.20. 142: 7 a–143: 1 b with 54: 4 b.
(impv p n-s with impv p-N-s)[40]
Ps. *54* did not form part of the starting group.
For Ps. *142:* 7 cf. G 3.10. and G 2.1.4.

For Ps. *143:* 1 cf. G 3.2.

The structure and contents of 142: 7–8 and 143: 1–4 are different: in the former the exhortations ("listen", "save" ×2) and motivations (ki with perf) are evenly distributed, in the latter the exhortations ("listen" ×2, "answer", "do not come") are found in the first part of the section, and the more substantial motivations concentrated at the end.

3.21. 5: 9 a–27: 11 b
(impv-s p-N p n-s)[41]
None of the psalms formed part of the starting group.

3.22. 22: 21 a–142: 8 a with 143: 11 b
(impv p-n n-s with impf p-n n-s)[42]
For Ps. *22:* 21 cf. G 3.15.
For Ps. *142:* 8 cf. G 3.10, 2.1.4.
For Ps. *143:* 11 cf. G 3.10, 1.1.1.
The expressions have similar function in context.

3.23. 71: 4 a–140: 5 a
(impv-s p-n+n)[43]
For Ps. *71:* 4 cf. G 3.1.
For Ps. *140:* 5 cf. G 2.2.6.
The expressions have similar function in context.

3.24–30. (cf. above G 3)[44] contain either no references at all to psalms from the starting group, or references to only one psalm, in which case there is no relevant material for comparison.

3.31. 38: 22 a–27: 9 e with 119: 8 b and 71: 9 b–71: 18 a
(neg v-s N with neg v-s x and x neg v-s)[45]
Pss. *38, 27* and *119* did not form part of the starting group; *71:* 9 b and 18 a remain, but two realizations of the same system within one unit could not provide criteria for isolating set phrases common to a group of psalms.

4. Formulaic clauses defining the relation YHWH—a third party are found in Culley's systems nrs 54, 141, 146, 162 and 163. None of these contain references to psalms from the starting group.

Under this heading I also include 17: 8–36: 8–57: 2 with 31: 21—61: 5,[46] where Pss. *17, 36* and *57* do not form part of the starting group, and Ps. *61:* 5 b contains cohortative sing—thus there is no relevant comparative material to Ps. *31:* 21 a.

# 5. Systematization and contextual remarks

5.1.1. Set phrases found in formulas or formulaic systems otherwise composed of material not belonging to the starting group: 6: 2 a, 5 a, (17: 8 b— cf. 2.2.5.), 18: 9 b, 10 a, 15 a–b, 19 b, 31 b, 35 a, 48 b, 25: 18 a, 61: 4 a, 71: 19 b, 86: 11 a, 15, 102: 13, 109: 1, 142: 5 a–b.

5.1.2. Formulas and formulaic systems without similar function in context: (13: 6–) 142: 8 d–116: 7 b, 18: 20 b–c – 22: 9 c–d, 17: 1 b–17: 1 c–17: 6 d–61: 2 a, 142: 7 a–143: 1 b.

5.1.3. Set phrases with differing functions within formulas and formulaic systems: 17: 13 d, 18: 49 c, 22: 10 a, 12 a, 25 c, 25: 5 c, 26: 1 a, 28: 1 a, 31: 16 b, 17 b, 40: 18 c, 69: 17 b, 109: 21 b (–c), 116: 2 a, 140: 7 b, 142: 4 b (cf. G 2.1.1.).

5.1.4. Two realizations of the same formula or formulaic system within the same unit were not seen as an indication of language characteristic of a group of psalms (69: 20 a, 6 a; 71: 9 a, 18 a latter part; 140: 2 b, 5 b). For Ps. 31: 21 a–61: 5 b with 17: 8 b cf. G 2.2.8.

5.2.1. Of 17 recorded groups of nominal formulaic clauses pertaining to YHWH, only three contained references to two or more psalms from the starting group. These three are the only ones initiated by ki; furthermore, the former two, (and Culley 122), are the only groups dealing with the relation between YHWH and the psalmist; the remaining formulas and formulaic systems report other aspects of divine attributes or functions. Within the groups 31: 5 b–71: 5 a and 71: 3 d–31: 4 a the expression formed one among several motivations for one among several exhortations, while in Ps. (63: 4 a–) 109: 21 b (–c) with (69: 17 (a–) b no set correlation between phrase and context could be established.

5.2.2. Formulas and formulaic systems containing verbal clauses with YHWH as subject and lacking a direct object were not to be found within the starting group.

Verbal clauses in the perfect, defining the relation between YHWH and the psalmist followed upon exhortations in concluding sections; the ki-clauses of Ps. 6: 9 b, 10 a, 116: 7 d, 8 a and 142: 8 d were preceded by impv, those of 56: 14 a and 86: 13 b by modal impfa, while 28: 6 b and 31: 23 d followed upon "bārūk"-statements.

Another function, namely summarizing the situation of the psalmist, was isolated for Ps. 69: 6 a and 142: 4 b.

56: 14 a–116: 8 a–86: 13 b were seen as having similar function in context.

57

5.2.3. The interpretation of clauses in impf 3sg, defining the relation between YHWH and the psalmist, was determined by the context.

5.2.4. Clauses in the imperative, addressed to YHWH and containing exhortations to "listen", were found at the outset of psalms or of new sections, characterized by a relatively large proportion of formulaic language: Ps. 28:2a, 31:3a, 61:2, 71:2c, 86:1a–b, 6, 102:2a, 3c, 142:7a, 143:1a, 1b; cf. also 17:1b, 1c, 6b, 6c and 88:3b in mainly non-formulaic contexts.

The above mentioned sections are followed by descriptions of a hostile third party in 17:10–12 and 28:3b–5, of personal misery in 88:6–10 and 102:4–12, of divine action and expressions of confidence in 31:6–9 and 61:5–6. Common to these is an almost total lack of formulaic language.

Clauses containing חנן and מלט/פלט were found in opening sections or at the outset of smaller units: Ps. 6:3a, 31:1, 2c, 10a, 56:2a, (71:4a), 86:3a and 116:4c. The exhortations are followed by descriptions of a hostile third party in Ps. 56:2b–3, of personal misery in 6:7–8 and 31:10b–14, of vows and expressions of confidence in 31:6–9 and 71:6–8—these descriptions are initiated by set phrases in Ps. 56:2b and 31:10b but otherwise show a remarkably small proportion of formulaic language. Other exhortations found in opening sections or at the outset of smaller units are those of Ps. 6:5a–b, 5c, 26:1a, 28:1a, 40:14b, 86:2a, 102:3d, 140:5a and 143:1c.

Ps. 22:20a, 20b, 25:16a, 40:14b, 69:17a–b, 71:12a, 12b, 86:12a–b, and 143:7a introduced concluding sections characterized by exhortations. Ps. 22:21a, 25:20a, (31:16b, 17a), 69:18b–c, 109:26b, 142:7c, 8a and 143:9a—all containing exhortations to "save"—were found within such sections. These units are followed by wishes concerning a third party in 40:15–16 and 71:13, by promises of praise and/or thanksgiving in 22:23 and 71:14, by ki and perf 2/3sg in 22:22, ki and a nominal clause in 143:12c (in 86:13 by ki with a nominal clause, and perf 2sg), ki and impf 2sg in 142:8d, and ki and perf 1sg in Ps. 25:21.

Similar functions in context were isolated for Ps. 31:3a–71:2c–102:3c–17:6c–86:1a–88:3b, 143:1a–102:2a, 86:6a–61:2a, 86:6b–28:2a, 25:16a–b–86:16a–b, 109:26b–6:5c, 142:7c–143:9a–18:18a, 31:10a–b–56:2a–b, 6:3a–b–6:3b–c–86:3a–b–69:17a–b, 25:20a–b–86:2a–b–6:5a–b–116:4b–c, 31:2c–71:2a–22:20b, 69:18b–c–102:3d–143:7a, 71:12b–22:20b, 22:21a–142:8a–143:11b, 71:4a–140:5a.

5.2.5. Formulas and formulaic systems defining the relation between YHWH and a third party had no relevance for psalms within the starting group.

H. 1. Formulas and formulaic systems, pertaining to a third party, without references to the psalmist or to YHWH, are present in the following groups: 31:7–Jon. 2:9, 134:1–135:2; 35:21–40:16; 9:16–31:5; 40:4–52:8; 79:10–115:2–Jo. 2:17; 118:2–124:1–129:1; 113:1a–135:1b and 113:1b–135:1a; 48:12–97:8; 34:15–37:27; 34:17–109:15.

1.1. 31:7–Jon. 2:9
(ptc n+n)[1]
In Ps. *31* the expression forms the object to a perf 1sg and has no relevance under this heading; thus there is no comparative material to *Jon. 2:9*.

1.2.–11. (cf. Culley nos. 158, 94, 100, 161, 62, 71, 113, 149, 144, 160) either lack references to psalms from the starting group or, when such references are present, do not contain comparative material.

2. Formulas and formulaic phrases, pertaining to a third party and containing references to the psalmist show perf 3sg, impf 3sg or perf 3pl.

2.1. Verbal clauses in perf 3sg are present in 7:6–143:3, 143:3–Lm. 3:6; 35:16–37:12.

2.1.1. 7:6a–c – 143:3a–b
(v n n-s v p-n p-n n-s)[2]
Ps. *7* did not form part of the starting group and thus there is no relevant comparative material to *143:* 3a–b.

2.1.2. 143:3c–Lm. 3:6
(impv-s p-n p-n+n)[3]
*Lm.* did not form part of the starting group and thus there is no relevant comparative material to *143:* 3c.

2.1.3. 35:16b–37:12b
(V p-s n-s)[4]
None of the psalms formed part of the starting group.

2.2. Verbal clauses in impf 3sg are present in 71:13a–b–35:4a–b–40:15a–b–35:26a–b—cf. also (6:11a–83:18b and) 35:4c–d–40:15c–d, and 35:26c–71:13c.
(impf 3pl c-impf 3 pl N+n-s with impf 3pl n c-impf 3pl N+n-s and impf 3pl n c-n x)[5]
Ps. *35* did not form part of the starting group.
Ps. *71:* 13 forms the conclusion of a section (vv. 9–11/12–13, cf. above n. F 38), initiated by exhortations (v. 9), motivated by <u>ki</u>-clauses referring to a

hostile third party (vv. 10–11), v. 12 contains further exhortations, which introduce the modal impfa of v. 13.

In Ps. *40* the modal impfa of vv. 15–16 are preceded by exhortations.

The expressions are seen as having similar function in context.

2.3. Verbal clauses in perf 3pl are present in 140: 6–119: 110–142: 4; 38: 20–69: 5–18: 5–116: 3 a with 18: 6 and possible variant system in 18: 6–109: 3— cf. also 116: 3 b; Lm. 2: 16–Lm. 3: 46–22: 14 with variant in 35: 21; Jon. 2: 6–69: 2; 42: 8–Jon. 2: 4.

2.3.1. 140: 6 a–119: 110 a–142: 4 d.

(v n n p-s)[6]

Ps. *119* did not form part of the starting group.

In Ps. *140* v. 6 a is preceded by exhortations with references to a third party (v. 5 a–b) and by a description of their activities (v. 5 c, in the perf); this description is continued throughout v. 6.

In Ps. *142* the expression is found in a section (vv. 4 c–5, cf. above n. F 14) describing misery. v. 4 b–c are not preceded by exhortations, and the plural category of v. 4 b is not defined.

The expressions are not seen as having similar function in context.

2.3.2. 38: 20 b–69: 5 a – cf. also 69: 5 b and 69: 5 a–40: 13 d

(perf 3pl ptc-s x with perf 3pl ptc-s x and perf 3pl p-n+n-s)[7]

Pss. *38* and *40:* 1–13 did not form part of the starting group, and thus there is no relevant comparative material to Ps. *69:* 5.

2.3.3. 18: 5 a–116: 3 a and 18: 6 b, 18: 6 a–109: 3 a with 116: 3 b

(perf 3pl-s n+n and perf 3pl-s n+n, n+n perf 3pl-s with n+n perf 3 pl-s)[8]

In Ps. *18* the expressions are found in a section (vv. 5–6, cf. above n. F 59) describing misery. This section is preceded by an "introit", expressing confidence (vv. 2–4), and followed by a description of invocation (v. 7 a–b), and exhortations (cf. F 2.6).

In Ps. *116* the expressions are found in a section (v. 3, cf. above n. F 9) describing misery. This section is preceded by a motivated expression of confidence (vv. 1–2) and followed by a description of invocation (v. 4 a), and an exhortation.

In Ps. *109* the expression is found in a section (vv. 1–5, cf. above n. F 5) initiated by an exhortation (v. 1), which is motivated by references to the activities of a third party (vv. 2–5). The following section (vv. 6–20) contains mainly modal impfa.

Ps. 18: 5 a, 6 a, 6 b and 116: 3 a, 3 b are seen as having similar function in context; from this differs Ps. 109: 3 a.

2.3.4. Lm. 2: 16a–Lm. 3: 46a–22: 14a with 35: 21a.

(v p-s n-s with v p-s n-s)[9]

*Lm.* and Ps. *35* did not form part of the starting group and thus there is no relevant comparative material to Ps. *22:* 14a.

2.3.5. Jon. 2: 6a–69: 2b

(v n p n)[10]

For *Jon. 2* cf. above n. F 15.

In Ps. *69* v. 2b constitutes the motivation to the initial exhortation. The "water"-motif of v. 2b is also present in v. 3, while v. 4 gives the somewhat surprising information that the throat of the psalmist is dry/hoarse; another aspect of the personal misery is given in v. 5—here with references to a third party.

Jon. 2: 6 is part of a review, Ps. 69: 2 represents the motivation for an exhortation—the expressions do not have similar function in context.

2.3.6. 42: 8b–Jon. 2: 4c

(n+n-s c-n-s p-s v)[11]

Ps. *42* did not form part of the starting group, and thus there is no relevant comparative material to *Jon. 2:* 4c.


3. The relation between a third party and YHWH is expressed in clauses in the imperative in Culley nrs 48, 49, 50, 51, 52, 72, 114, 115, 116, 117, 118, 119, 123 and 148. Of these, only the groups 50, 116 and 148 contain material from the starting group: 33: 2–98: 5–147: 7 with 9: 12–30: 5; 30: 5–90: 7; 35: 27–40: 17, but as Pss. 33, 98, 147, 9, 90 and 35 do not constitute relevant comparative material an analysis is superfluous.

Under this heading I also include Culley 150 (5: 12–9: 11), 167 (98: 3–Is. 52: 10) and 68 (73: 27–83: 3–92: 10) without references to the starting group.


4. Systematization and contextual remarks.

4.1.1. Set phrases found in formulas or formulaic systems otherwise composed of material not belonging to the starting group: 22: 14a, 30: 5a, 5b, 31: 5a (latter part), 40: 16 (latter part), 17b, 69: 5a, 5b, 109: 15b, 143: 3a–b, 3c and Jon. 2: 4c.

4.1.2. Formulaic systems without similar function in context: 140: 6a–142: 4d, Jon. 2: 6a–69: 2b.

4.1.3. Set phrases with different functions within formulas and formulaic systems: 109: 3a.

4.1.4. The formula 31: 7–Jon. 2: 9 had no relevance under this heading.

4.2. Formulas or formulaic systems pertaining to a third party, and lacking references to the psalmist or to YHWH, were non-existent within the starting group. The relation between a third party and the psalmist was expressed in formulaic verbal clauses in perf 3sg, impf 3sg or perf 3pl; the relation between a third party and YHWH was mainly articulated in exhortations to praise—such formulas and formulaic systems were non-existent within the starting group.

4.2.1. Formulas or formulaic systems containing verbal clauses in perf 3sg were not found within the starting group. One formulaic system, containing verbal clauses in impf 3sg, was found within the starting group; the expressions in Ps. 71: 13 and 40: 15, preceded by exhortations, were interpreted as modal.

4.2.2. The verbal clauses in perf 3pl are preceded or followed by exhortations, and form part of motivating descriptions of the activities of a hostile third party. Such descriptions usually comprise several stanzas, show few instances of formulaic language and contain mainly verbal clauses in the perfect (18: 5–6, 22: 12–19, 69: 2–5, 116: 3–4, 140: 5–6, 142: 4 b–5, Jon. 2: 4, 6).

Only Ps. 18: 5 a, 6 a, 6 b–116: 3 a, 3 b formed a system with similar function in context.

# J. APPLICATION TO PARTICULAR PSALMS

1.1. Psalm 6 was divided into sections 2–6, 7–8 and 9–11 (cf. above n. F 26).

Within vv. 2–6 formulaic language is present in vv. 2, 3 a–b, 3 c–d, 5 a–b and 5 c. Apart from v. 2, which constituted a system together with Ps. 38: 2, these clauses showed similarities to other smaller units within the starting group: 6: 3 a–b – 6: 3 c–d – 86: 3 a–b – 69: 17 a–b, 6: 5 a–b – 25: 20 a–b – 86: 2 a–b (–116: 4 b–c) and 6: 5 c–109: 26 b.

vv. 7–8 contain only one example of formulaic language, i.e. v. 8 a, which showed certain similarities to Ps. 31: 10 c.

vv. 9–11 contain formulaic language in v. 9 b, 10 a and 11 a. v. 9 b and 10 a were listed as variants in the perf to clauses in the impv, but as such they showed a function similar to other clauses in the perf (cf. G 3.3, 3.6 and 2.1). v. 11 a was compared with Ps. 83: 18 a—the two presenting certain similarities to 71: 13 a–b – 35: 4 a–b – 40: 15 a–b – 35: 26 a–b (cf. H 2.2).

1.2. Psalm 17 was divided into the sections 1–6 b, 6 c–12, 13–14 and 15 (cf. above n. G 21).

vv. 1–6 b contain formulaic language in v. 1 b and 1 c. These clauses formed part of a system for which no common function in context could be isolated.

vv. 6 c–12 contain formulaic language in v. 6 c, 6 d and 8 b. v. 6 c showed similarities to Ps. 31: 3 a–71: 2 c–102: 3 c–86: 1 a and 88: 3 b, v. 6 d formed part of a system for which no common function in context could be isolated, and v. 8 b lacked comparative material within the starting group.

vv. 13–14 contain only one example of formulaic language, i.e. v. 13 d, which differed from the other members of its group concerning function in context.

v. 15 lacks formulaic language.

1.3. Psalm 18 was divided into the sections 2–4, 5–6, 7+17–20 b, 20 c, 8–16, 21–25, 26–30/31, 31/32–46, 47–49, 50 and 51 (cf. above n. F 59).

vv. 2–4 lack formulaic language (cf., however, Culley no. 176, p. 91).

v. 5–6 contain formulaic language in v. 5 a, 6 a and 6 b. These clauses were judged to have a function in context similar to that of Ps. 116: 3 a, 3 b.

vv. 7+17–20 b (–c) contain formulaic language in v. 7 d, 18, 19 b and

20 b–c. v. 7 d formed a system with similar function in context together with Ps. 88: 3 a and 102: 2 b, v. 18 with 142: 7 c and 143: 9 a, while v. 19 b (and 48 b) lacked relevant comparative material within the starting group, and vv. 20 b–c formed part of a system for which no common function in context could be isolated.

vv. 8–16 contain formulaic language in v. 8 a, 9 b, 10 a, 11 c and 15 a—all of them bound in formulas or formulaic systems with psalms not belonging to the starting group.

vv. 21–25 lack formulaic language.

vv. 26–30/31 contain only one example of formulaic language, i.e. vv. 31 b–c, which constituted a system together with Pr. 30: 5.

vv. 31/32–46 contain (apart from v. 31 b–c) only one example of formulaic language, i.e. v. 35 a, which constituted a formula together with Ps. 144: 1 b.

vv. 47–49 contain formulaic language in v. 48 b and 49 c. v. 48 b lacked comparative material within the starting group, v. 49 c formed part of a system for which no common function in context could be isolated.

v. 50 a formed a system with similar function in context together with Ps. 86: 12 a.

v. 51 lacks formulaic language.

1.4. Psalm 22 was divided into the sections 2–11 (2–3, 4–6, 7–9, 10–11), 12–17/18–19, 20–22 a, 22 b, 23, 24–25, 26, 27, 28–29, 30–32 (cf. above n. F 56).

vv. 2–11 contain formulaic language in v. 9 c–d and 10 a. vv. 9 c–d formed part of a system for which no common function in context could be isolated, v. 10 a differed from the other members of its group concerning function in context.

vv. 12–16/17–19 contain formulaic language in v. 12 a and 14 a. v. 12 a differed from the other members of its group, v. 14 a lacked relevant comparative material within the starting group.

vv. 20–22 a contain formulaic language in v. 20 a, 20 b and 21 a. v. 20 a formed a system with similar function in context together with Ps. 71: 12 a; v. 20 b showed similarities to Ps. 40: 14 b and 71: 12 b, v. 21 a to Ps. 142: 8 a and 143: 11 b.

v. 22 b lacks formulaic language.

v. 23 a formed a system with similar function in context together with Ps. 86: 12 b.

vv. 24–25 contain only one example of formulaic language, i.e. v. 25 c, which differed from the other members of its group concerning function in context.

vv. 27, 28–29/30–32 lack formulaic language.

1.5. Psalm 25 was divided into the sections 1, 2–3, 4–7, 8–11, 12–15, 16–21, 22 (cf. above n. F 6).

v. 1 differed from the other members of its group concerning function in context.

vv. 2–3 contain formulaic language in vv. 2 a–b, which differed from the other members of its group concerning function in context.

vv. 4–7 contain formulaic language in v. 5 c, which differed from the other members of its group concerning function in context.

vv. 8–11 and 12–15 lack formulaic language.

vv. 16–21 contain formulaic language in vv. 16 a–b, 16 c, 18 a, 20 a–b and 20 c–d. vv. 16 a–b showed similarities to Ps. 86: 16 a–b concerning function in context, vv. 20 a–b to 86: 2 a–b (and 116: 4 b–c, 6: 5 a–b), while v. 16 c formed part of a system for which no common function in context could be isolated, v. 18 a lacked comparative material within the starting group, and vv. 20 c–d differed from the other members of its group concerning function in context.

v. 22 lacks formulaic language.

1.6. Psalm 26 was divided into the sections 1, 2–3, 4–8, 9–11 and 12 (cf. above n. F 46).

v. 1 a–b and 1 c–d contain formulaic language. vv. 1 a–b differed from the other members of its group, vv. 1 c–d formed part of a system for which no common function in context could be isolated.

vv. 2–3 contain formulaic language in v. 3 b, which lacked comparative material within the starting group.

vv. 4–8 contain formulaic language in v. 6 a and 7 b, both of them lacking comparative material within the starting group.

vv. 9–11 and 12 lack formulaic language.

1.7. Psalm 28 was divided into the sections 1–2, 3–4/5, 6–7, 8/9 (cf. above n. F 48).

vv. 1–2 contain formulaic language in v. 1 a, 1 b, 1 d and 2 a. v. 1 a was collated with Ps. 30: 9 a and 61: 3 a, v. 1 d with 143: 7 d, v. 2 a with 86: 6 b, while v. 1 b differed from the other members of its group concerning function in context.

vv. 3–4/5 lack formulaic language.

vv. 6–7 contain formulaic language in v. 6 b, which was collated with Ps. 31: 23 c and 6: 9 b (cf. G 3.6).

vv. 8/9 lack formulaic language.

1.8. Psalm 30 was divided into the sections 2–4, 5–6, 9–13 and 7–8 (cf. above n. F 22).

vv. 2–4 contain formulaic language in v. 3a, which was collated with Ps. 28: 1a and 61: 3a.

vv. 5–6 contain formulaic language in v. 5a and 5b, both of them lacking comparative material within the starting group.

vv. 7–8 contain formulaic language in v. 7a and 7b; the former was collated with Jon. 2: 5a, the latter lacked comparative material.

vv. 9–13 contain formulaic language in v. 9a, which was brought together with Ps. 28: 1a and 61: 3a.

1.9. Psalm 31 was divided into the sections 2a–b, 2c–5, 6–7, 8–9, 10–14, 15–18b (18c–19), 20–21, 22, 23 and 24–25 (cf. above n. F 17).

vv. 2a–b were collated with Ps. 71: 1.

vv. 2c–5 contain formulaic language in v. 2c, 3a, 4a, 5a and 5b. v. 2c was brought together with Ps. 71: 2a and 143: 1c, v. 3a with 71: 2c, 102: 3c, 17: 6c, 86: 1a and 88: 3b, v. 4a with 71: 3d, 5b with 71: 5a, while v. 5a lacked comparative material.

vv. 6–7 contain formulaic language in v. 7a, which lacked comparative material (cf. H 1.1).

vv. 8–9 contain formulaic language in vv. 8a–b, which lacked comparative material (cf. F 2.3.3).

vv. 10–14 contain formulaic language in vv. 10a(–b), 10b, 10c, 11a–b and 14a–b. v. 10a(–b) was brought together with Ps. 56: 2a(–b), v. 10c with 6: 8(?), 11a with 102: 4a, while v. 10b was found in a system for which no common function in context could be isolated, and vv. 14a–b lacked comparative material.

vv. 15–18b (18c–19) contain formulaic language in v. 15b, 16b and 17b. v. 15b was collated with Ps. 142: 6b, while v. 16b and 17b differed from their groups concerning function in context.

vv. 20–21 contain formulaic language in v. 21a, which lacked comparative material (cf. G 2.2.8).

vv. 22–23 contain formulaic language in vv. 23a–b and 23c–d—the former were brought together with Ps. 116: 11a, the latter with 6: 9b and 28: 6b (cf. G 3.6).

vv. 24–25 contain formulaic language in vv. 25a–b, which lacked comparative material.

1.10. Psalm 40 (cf. F 1.1.1) might be divided into the sections 14–17 and 18.

vv. 14–17 contain formulaic language in vv. 14b, 15a–b, 15c–d, 16aβ and 17. v. 14b was collated with Ps. 71: 12b and 22: 20b, v. 15 with 71: 13, while v. 16aβ and 17 lacked comparative material.

v. 18a was brought together with Ps. 69: 30a, v. 18c differed from the other members of its group concerning function in context.

1.11. Psalm 56 was divided into the sections 2–3 (4?), 5, 6–7, 8, 9/10–11, 12 and 13–14 (cf. above n. F 45).

vv. 2–3 (4) contain formulaic language in vv. 2 a–b, which was collated with Ps. 31: 10 a (–b).

v. 5 (and 12) were compared with Ps. 118: 6, outside the starting group, vv. 5 b–c (and 12 a–b) belonged to a system for which no common function in context could be isolated (cf. F 2.1.5).

vv. 6–7, 8, 9/10–11 lack formulaic language.

v. 14 a was brought together with Ps. 116: 8 a and 86: 13 b.

1.12. Psalm 61 was divided into the sections 2–3 c, 3 d–4, 5–6, 7–8 and 9 (cf. above n. F 49).

vv. 2–3 c contain formulaic language in v. 2 a, 2 b and 3 a. v. 2 a was collated with Ps. 86: 6 a, v. 3 a with 30: 9 a and 28: 1 a, while v. 2 b formed part of a system for which no common function in context could be isolated.

vv. 3 d–4 contain formulaic language in v. 4 a, which lacked comparative material.

vv. 5–6 contain formulaic language in v. 5 b, which lacked comparative material (cf. G 2.2.8).

vv. 7–8 lack formulaic language.

v. 9 a differed from the other members of its group concerning function in context.

1.13. Psalm 69 was divided into the sections 2–6, 7, 8, 9–13, 14–16, 17–20, 21–22, 23–29, 30, 31, 32, 33–34, 35–37 (cf. above n. F 7).

vv. 2–6 contain formulaic language in v. 2 b, 5 a, 5 b and 6 a. v. 2 b formed part of a system for which no common function in context could be isolated, v. 5 a and 5 b lacked comparative material (cf. H 2.3.2). For v. 6 a cf. G 2.1.1.

vv. 7, 8, 9–13 and 14–16 lack formulaic language.

vv. 17–20 contain formulaic language in vv. 17 a–b, 17 (a–) b, 18 a, 18 b–c and 20 a. vv. 17 a–b were collated with Ps. 6: 3 a–b, 3 c–d and 86: 3 a–b, v. 18 a with 102: 3 a and 143: 7 c, vv. 18 b–c with 102: 3 e and 143: 7 a, while v. 17 (a–) b and 20 a (cf. G 1.1.1) were found in systems for which no common function in context could be isolated.

vv. 21–22, 23–29, 31, 32, 33–34 and 35–37 lack formulaic language.

v. 30 a was brought together with Ps. 40: 18 a.

1.14. Psalm 71 was divided into the sections 1, 2–5, 6–8, 9–11, 12–13, 14–15, 16–19 a, 19 b–20 b, 20 c–21, 22, 23–24 a and 24 b (cf. above n. F 38).

v. 1 was collated with Ps. 31: 2 a–b.

vv. 2–5 contain formulaic language in v. 2 a, 2 c, 3 d, 4 a and 5 a. v. 2 a was brought together with Ps. 31:2c and 143:1c, v. 2c with 31:3a, 102:3c, 17c, 86:1a and 88:3b, v. 3d with 31:4a, v. 4a with 140:5a, and v. 5a with 31:5b.

vv. 6–8 lack formulaic language.

vv. 9–11 contain formulaic language in v. 9b, which lacked comparative material (cf. G 3.31).

vv. 12–13 contain formulaic language in v. 12a and 13—the former was collated with Ps. 22:20a, the latter with 40:15.

vv. 14–15 lack formulaic language.

vv. 16–19a contain formulaic language in v. 18a, which lacked comparative material (cf. G 3.31).

vv. 19–20b contain formulaic language in v. 19b, which lacked comparative material.

vv. 20c–21 lack formulaic language.

22a differed from the other members of its group concerning function in context.

vv. 23–24a contain formulaic language in v. 24a, which lacked comparative material.

v. 24b may be compared with v. 13 (cf. Culley, no. 40, p. 54ff.).

1.15. Psalm 86 was divided into the sections 1–5, 6–8, 9–10, 11–13, 14–15 and 16–17 (cf. above n. F 3).

vv. 1–5 contain formulaic language in vv. 1a–b, 1c, 2a–b, 3a(–b), 3b and 4b.

vv. 1a–b were collated with Ps. 31:3a, 71:2c, 17:6c and 88:3b, v. 1c with 25:16c, vv. 2a–b with 25:20a–b, 6:5 a–b (and 116:4b–c), v. 3a(–b) with 31:10a–b and 69:17a–b, v. 4b with 143:8d, while v. 3b differed from the other members of its system concerning function in context.

vv. 6–8 contain formulaic language in v. 6a and 6b—the former was brought together with Ps. 61:2a, the latter with 28:2a.

vv. 9–10 lack formulaic language.

vv. 11–13 contain formulaic language in v. 11a, 11b, 12a, 12b and 13b. v. 12a was collated with Ps. 18:50a, v. 12b with 22:23a, 13b with 56:14a and 116:8a, while v. 11a and 11b lacked comparative material.

vv. 14–15 contain formulaic language in v. 15, which lacked comparative material.

vv. 16–17 contain formulaic language in vv. 16a–b, which were brought together with Ps. 25:16a–b.

1.16. Psalm 88 was divided into the sections 2/3–10a, 10b–13 and 14–19 (cf. above n. F 50).

vv. 2/3–10a contain formulaic language in v. 3a, 3b and 5a. v. 3a was brought together with Ps. 102:2b and 18:7d, v. 3b with 31:3a, 71:2c, 102:3c and 17:6c, while v. 5a differed from the other members of its group concerning function in context.

vv. 10b–13 lack formulaic language.

vv. 14–19 contain formulaic language in v. 14a and 15—the former differed from the other members of its group concerning function in context, the latter lacked comparative material.

1.17. Psalm 102 was divided into the sections 2–4/5–12, 13–23, 24–25b, and 25c–29 (cf. above n. F 30).

vv. 2–12 contain formulaic language in v. 2a, 2b, 3a, 3b, 3c, 3e and 4a. v. 2a was collated with Ps. 143:1a, v. 2b with 88:3a and 18:7d, v. 3a with 69:18a and 143:7c, v. 3c with 31:3a, 71:2c, 17:6c, 86:1a and 88:3b, v. 3e with 69:18b–c and 143:7a, v. 4a with 31:11a, while v. 3b lacked comparative material.

vv. 13–23 contain formulaic language in v. 13, which lacked comparative material.

vv. 24, 25 and 26–29 lack formulaic language.

1.18. Psalm 109 was divided into the sections 1–5, 6–20, 21–25/26–27, 28–29, 30 and 31 (cf. above n. F 5).

vv. 1–5 contain formulaic language in v. 1 and 3a—the former lacked comparative material, the latter differed from the other members of its group concerning function in context. vv. 6–20 contain formulaic language in v. 15b, which lacked comparative material.

vv. 21–27 contain formulaic language in v. 21b(–c), 22a, 22b, and 26b. v. 26b was collated with Ps. 6:5c, while v. 21b(–c) formed part of a system for which no common function could be isolated, v. 22a differed from the other members of its group concerning function in context, and v. 22b lacked comparative material.

vv. 28–29, 30 and 31 lack formulaic language.

1.19. Psalm 116 was divided into the sections 1–2, 3a–b, 3c–4, 5–6, 7–8, 9, 10–11, 12–14, 15, 16a–c, 17–18 and 19 (cf. above n. F 9).

vv. 1–2 contain formulaic language in v. 2a, which differed from the other members of its group concerning function in context.

v. 3a, 3b were collated with Ps. 18:5a, 6a and 6b.

vv. 3c–4 contain formulaic language in vv. 4b–c, which were collated with Ps. 25:20a–b, 86:2a–b and 6:5a–b.

vv. 5–6 lack formulaic language.

vv. 7–8 contain formulaic language in v. 7b and 8a—v. 7b formed part of a system for which no common function could be isolated, v. 8a was brought together with Ps. 56: 14a and 86: 13b.

v. 9 lacks formulaic language.

vv. 10–11 contain formulaic language in v. 11a, which was brought together with Ps. 31: 23a.

vv. 12–14, 15 lack formulaic language.

v. 16b formed part of a system for which no common function could be isolated.

vv. 16d, 17–18 and 19 lack formulaic language.

1.20. Psalm 140 was divided into the sections 2–4, 5–6, 7–8, 9–12, 13 and 14 (cf. above n. F 40).

vv. 2–4 contain formulaic language in v. 2b, which formed part of a system for which no common function could be isolated.

vv. 5–6 contain formulaic language in v. 5a, 5b and 6a. v. 5a was collated with Ps. 71: 4a, while v. 5b and 6a formed part of systems for which no common functions could be isolated.

vv. 7–8 contain formulaic language in v. 7a and 7b—both differing from the other members of its system concerning function in context.

vv. 9–12, 13 and 14 lack formulaic language.

1.21. Psalm 142 was divided into the sections 2–4b, 4c–5, 6 and 7–8 (cf. above n. F 14).

vv. 2–4b contain formulaic language in v. 2a, 2b, 4a and 4b. v. 2a and 2b lacked comparative material, v. 4a belonged to a system for which no common function could be isolated, and 4b differed from the other members of its group concerning function in context.

vv. 4c–5 contain formulaic language in vv. 4c, 4d, and 5a–b. v. 4c and 4d belonged to systems for which no common function could be isolated, vv. 5a–b lacked comparative material.

v. 6a differed from the other members of its group concerning function in context, v. 6b was collated with Ps. 31: 15b.

vv. 7–8 contain formulaic language in v. 7a, 7b, 7c(–d), 8a and 8d. v. 7c(–d) was brought together with Ps. 143: 9a and 18: 18a, v. 8a with 22: 21a and 143: 11b, while v. 7b lacked comparative material, and v. 7a and 7a and 8d differed from the other members of their groups concerning function in context.

1.22. Psalm 143 was divided into the sections 1–4, 5–6, 7–10b and 10c–12 (cf. above n. F 12).

vv. 1–4 contain formulaic language in vv. 1a, 1b, 1c, 3a–b, 3c and 4a. v. 1a was brought together with 102: 2a, v. 1c with 31: 2c and 71: 2a, while

vv. 3 a–b and 3 c lacked comparative material, and v. 1 b and 4 a belonged to systems for which no common function in context could be isolated.

vv. 5–6 contain formulaic language in v. 5 a, 5 b and 5 c, all of them lacking comparative material.

vv. 7–10 b contain formulaic language in v. 7 a, 7 c, 7 d, 8 a, 8 b, 8 c, 8 d, 9 a, 10 b. v. 7 a was brought together with Ps. 69: 18 b–c and 102: 3 e, v. 7 b with 69: 18 a and 102: 3 a, v. 7 d with 28: 1 d, 8 d, with 86: 4 b, 9 a with 142: 7 c and 18: 18 a, while v. 8 a lacked comparative material, and v. 8 b, 8 c and 10 b differed from the other members of their groups concerning function in context.

vv. 10 c–12 contain formulaic language in v. 11 b and 12 c—the former was brought together with Ps. 22: 21 a and 142: 8 a, the latter belonged to a system for which no common function in context could be isolated.

2. An "average psalm" belonging to the assumpted group would have 45 % of its set phrases bound in formulas/formulaic systems with other smaller units from the starting group, showing a function in context similar to these, 27 % in formulas/ systems with smaller units outside the starting group, 14 % showing differing function from the other members of the formula/ system, and 13 % bound in formulas/systems without similar function in context (cf. Appendix II).

2.1. Psalms 18 and 30 show a remarkably high degree of set phrases bound in formulas/systems with smaller units outside the starting group, Pss. 22 and 88 have one third or more of the set phrases showing differing function in context; 40 % of the set phrases of Ps. 69 are bound in formulas/ systems without common function (cf. also Ps. 116), while Pss. 17, 25, 26, 56, 109, 140 and 142 diverge from the "ideal" pattern at more than one point (cf. Appendix II).

2.1.1. In Ps. 18 five of the nine set phrases bound in formulas/systems with smaller units not belonging to the starting group are found in the section 8–16. It has been pointed out above (n. F 63) that this section disrupts the themes of v. 7 and 17 ff. of the "lament" proper.

In Ps. 30 two of the three set phrases lacking comparative material within the starting group are found in the introductory summary (vv. 2–4), and one in the transitional section 7–8. The "lament" (vv. 9–13), which contains only one instance of formulaic language has little relevance in an investigation of formulaic language.

2.1.2. Psalms 22 and 88 show a high degree of set phrases which differ from other members of formulas/systems concerning function in context. This could probably provide a basis for diachronic speculations—I shall, however, for the time being, abstain from such theories, as this investigation is still on a rather mechanical level and does not yet yield sufficient criteria for generative reasoning.

2.1.3. For comments on the formulas/systems of Ps. 69 (and 116), for which no common function in context could be isolated cf. above 2.1.2.

2.1.4. Psalms 17, 25, 26, 56, 109, 140 and 142 diverged from the "ideal" pattern at more than one point. Common to all of them is a low percentage of phrases with set relations to the starting group: Pss. 26 and 109 show many references to units outside this group, Pss. 25, 109, 140 and 142 have high proportions of set phrases differing in function from other members of formulas/systems, Pss. 17, 56 and 140 show formulaic language bound in groups for which no common function in context could be isolated.

These seven psalms differ formally from the tendency within the starting group—this is, however, not a sufficient reason to exclude them from the investigation: formulaic similarities alone do not provide criteria for "Gattungsbestimmung" but should be combined with similarities on a locutionary level.[1] Therefore, my next step will be an attempt to isolate a "Strukturmuster"[2] or "basic pattern" common to a group of psalms.

# K. IN SEARCH FOR A BASIC COMPOSITIONAL PATTERN

1.1.1. Psalms 18: 2–4, 22: 2–11, 25: 1, 26: 1, 28: 1–2, 30: 9,[1] 31: 2 a–b, 61: 2–3 c, 71: 1, (88: 2, 10 b–c, 14),[2] 116: 1–2 and 142: 2–4 b present introductions in the form of reviews, summaries or descriptions of the invocational situation. These are followed by exhortations with motivations in Ps. 31: 2 c–5, 61: 3 d–4, and 71: 2–5 (cf. also 28: 3–5), and by exhortations leading into detailed descriptions of personal misery in 22: 12–17/18–19 (and 88: 3–10 a; cf. also 26: 2–3/4–8, 9–11, dealing with blamelessness).

Psalms 18: 5–6, 7 a–b with 17–20, and 116: 3 a–b, 3 c–4 a contain descriptions of distress and invocational situation followed by exhortations. These are motivated by ki-clauses in 18: 18 c and 20 c, while 116: 5–6 show hymnic traits. Ps. 25: 2–3 contain general expressions of confidence, followed by exhortations with references to YHWH's attributes (vv. 4–7) and two "general" sections with related terminology (vv. 8–11, 12–15—cf. above n. F 6), Ps. 142: 4 c–5 describe a situation of want, followed by a transition (v. 6) and exhortations with motivations (v. 7–8 b); Ps. 30: 9 and 88: 10 b–c, 14 are followed by questions, addressed to YHWH (30: 10, 88: 11–13, 15)— Ps. 30: 10 introduces exhortations without motivations (v. 11).

1.1.2. Psalms 6, 17, 40: 14–18, 56, 69, 86, 102, 109, 140 and 143 open with exhortations. Psalms 6: 2–6 and 86: 1–5 contain evenly distributed exhortations and motivations (cf. also 143: 1–4); in Ps. 69: 2–6, 102: 2–4/5–12 and 109: 1–5 the exhortations introduce detailed descriptions of personal misery (cf. also 56: 2–3/4, 140: 2–4,5–6 dealing with a third party).

Psalms 40: 14 and 17: 1 are followed by modal impfa (40: 15–17, 17: 2).

1.2. Within the psalms sections containing exhortations[3] are found in Ps. 17: 6 c–12/13–14, 22: 12–17/18–19, 20–22 a, 25: 16–20 a, 31: 10–14, 69: 14–16, 17–20, 71: 9–11, 86: 6–8, 109: 21–25, 140: 9–13 and 143: 7–10 b.

Psalms 25: 16–20 a, 69: 17–20 and 143: 7–10 b show evenly distributed exhortations with motivating ki-clauses (cf. also 71: 9–11, 86: 6–8); in Ps. 22: 12–17/18–19, 31: 10–14 and 109: 21–25 the initial exhortations introduce detailed descriptions of personal misery. In 69: 14–16 and 22: 20–22 a the exhortations are devoid of motivations—the latter also lack descriptions of

73

misery. 140: 9–13 is unclear, and has only one reference to first person sing.

1.3. Leaving the "introductions" out of account, the opening sections can be divided into two main groups: one, consisting of Ps. 6: 2–6, 31: 2 c–5, 61: 3 d–4, 71: 2–5 and 86: 1–5 where exhortations and motivations (both mainly in formulaic language) are evenly distributed (cf. also 28: 3–5, 143: 1–4 and, within psalms, 25: 16–20 a, 69: 17–20, 143: 7–10 b with 71: 9–11 and 86: 6–8), and a second, consisting of Ps. 22: 12–17/18–19, 69: 2–6, 102: 2–4/5–12 and 109: 1–5 with exhortations leading into (mainly non-formulaic) descriptions of personal misery (cf. also 88: 3–10 a and, within psalms, 31: 10–14 and 109: 21–25).

1.3.1.1. In opening sections exhortations to "save" are most frequent within the first group (Ps. 31: 2, 71: 2, 4; 6: 5, 71: 2, 86: 2; 31: 3, 71: 2; 6: 5—cf. also 6: 3, 86: 3), followed by injunctions to "listen" (31: 3, 71: 2, 86: 1; 143: 1×2), and to "lead and keep" (31: 4×2, 61: 3, 86: 2)—others are "be" (31: 3, 71: 3), "answer" (86: 1, 143: 1) "heal" (6: 3), "come back" (6: 5), "give reason to rejoice" (86: 4), "repay" (28: 4×2) and "let have" (28: 4).

Four negative commands are found: 6: 2×2 ("do not punish", "do not reprove"), 28: 3 ("do not drag") and 143: 2 ("do not put on trial").

Within the psalms the distribution is somewhat different; here exhortations dealing with "divine presence" are the most frequent (Ps. 25: 16, 69: 17; 69: 18, 143: 7; 71: 9×2), followed by summons to "listen" and "see" (69: 17, 18, 143: 7, 86: 6×2), to "save" (25: 20, 143: 9; 69: 19—cf. also 25: 16)—others are "forgive" (25: 18), "keep" (25: 20), "come to my side" (69: 19), "let hear/show" (143: 7) and "teach" (143: 10).

1.3.1.2. The motivations contain expressions of confidence (Ps. 31: 4, 5, 61: 4, 71: 3, 5, 86: 5, 143: 10), references to the character or attributes of YHWH (6: 5, 31: 4, 69: 17), and short statements concerning the situation, character or actions of the psalmist (6: 2, 3 f., 86: 1, 2, 25: 16 f., 69: 18, 19, 143: 7; 86: 3, 4, 25: 20, 143: 8, 9).

1.3.2.1. In the second group the majority of the exhortations deal with "listening"—"answering" (Ps. 102: 3, 88: 3, 102: 2, 38: 3; 102: 2; 109: 1; 102: 3), two with "divine presence" (22: 12, 102: 3) and only one with "saving" (69: 2). Within the psalms injunctions to "take pity" (31: 10), "defend" and "rescue" (109: 21) are found.

In this group most of the exhortations lack first person sing suffixes, which should be compared to the relative frequency of such suffixes within the first group.

1.3.2.2. The motivations contain references to the miserable state of the psalmist (22: 15–16, 69: 4, 102: 4, 5–8, 10, 12, 88: 4–7, 10 and, within psalms, 31: 10b–14, 109: 22–25), caused by human enemies (22: 18–19, 69: 5, 102: 9, 109: 2–5; 31: 14), "animals" (22: 13–14), "water" (69: 2–3), forsakenness (22: 12, 88: 9), and/or divine wrath (88: 8, 102: 11).

Expressions of confidence and references to YHWH's attributes are lacking (cf., however, 109: 21).

2. Clauses in perf 2/3 sg with or without an initial ki, modal impfa 1sg, impfa 2/3 sg with or without an initial ki, and modal impfa 3pl with or without neg impfa 1sg have been ascribed a concluding function (cf. above F 4.2.5, and G 5.2.4).

2.1.1. The majority of the perf 2/3sg-clauses motivate exhortations and are initiated by ki: Ps. 6: 9b, 10a, 18: 20c, 28: 6b, 31: 22b, 61: 6, 86: 17c–d and 116: 7b, 8a (cf. also 109: 27b). The contexts[4] of 6: 9b, 10a and 86: 17c–d also contain modal impfa 3pl (6: 11, 86: 17b), while Ps. 28: 7, 61: 5 and 116: 9 show modal impfa 1sg; 31: 22c–23a indicate a situation (p-n).

Psalm 18: 20c concludes the "lament".

2.1.2. Psalms 31: 8c–9, 56: 14a and 86: 13b (31: 8c–9 lacking the initial ki) are preceded by, and closely associated with, modal impfa 1sg (31: 8a–b, 56: 13b, 86: 12).

2.1.3. Psalms 22: 22b and 30: 12, both lacking the initial ki, follow rather abruptly upon exhortations, and introduce modal impfa 1sg (22: 23, 30: 13).

2.2. Psalms 17: 15, 18: 50, 22: 26b, 26: 12b, 61: 9a, 69: 31, 71: 22, (23–24), and 109: 30 contain modal impfa 1sg (for other instances, combined with clauses in perf 2/3sg, cf. above). Ps. 18: 50, initiated by ʿal ken, is preceded by a hymnic section, and 61: 9, initiated by ken, by modal impfa. Ps. 17: 15, 22: 26, 26: 12, 71: 22, (23–24) and 109: 30 seem to stand isolated—109: 30 is, however, followed by ki and impf 3sg (with *third person sing* object).

2.3. Psalms 17: 6b, 86: 7b, 140: 13b and 142: 8d contain clauses in impf 2/3sg, initiated by ki (cf. also 25: 15b; for 109: 31a cf. above, for 69: 30a–b below 2.5.1.2). 17: 6b and 140: 13b are preceded by perf 1sg within the stanza, 86: 7b by impf 1sg and 142: 8d by impf 3pl. With the exception of 140: 13b the expressions conclude their sections (for Ps. 86: 8 cf. above n. F 3).

2.4. For modal impfa 3pl cf. 2.1.1 and 2.5.1.1. Cf. also Ps. 71: 13, preceded by exhortations, 71: 24 b in the perf, and further the relatively isolated 69: 7 and 109: 28 f.

2.5. Remaining smaller units within concluding passages could be divided into two main groups: statements pertaining to the psalmist, and statements involving a third party.

2.5.1. The first group is subdivided into ki-clauses with perf 1sg or nominals, and clauses containing modal impfa 2sg with first person sing objects. With the possible exception of Ps. 69: 30, such clauses are not combined with other concluding material (cf. above).

2.5.1.1. Psalms 25: 21 b, 31: 18 b and 69: 8 a contain ki with perf 1sg, 143: 12 c has ki with a nominal clause. Ps. 25: 21 b and 143: 12 c are preceded by modal impfa, 69: 8 a by negative commands, and 31: 18 b by neg impf 1sg (cf. also 25: 20 c). While 25: 21⁵ and 143: 12 conclude the psalms, 69: 7–8 seem to lack connexions in context; 31: 18 b is followed by modal impfa 3pl.

2.5.1.2. Psalms 40: 18 b and 69: 30 b show modal impf 3sg preceded by identical nominal clauses. 40: 18 b is followed by a nominal clause and a negative command, 69: 30 b by modal impfa 1sg.

2.5.2. The second group is subdivided into exhortations with or without motivations, addressed to specific categories, exhortations with or without motivations with a general address, and exhortations addressed to YHWH with the people and/or their king/Messiah as object.

2.5.2.1. Psalms 22: 27, 24–25 and 31: 24/25 belong to the first category (cf. also 69: /32/33–34, 140: 14). These sections are preceded by other concluding alternatives (cf. above).

2.5.2.2. Psalms 22: 28–29/30–32 and 69: 35–37 are initiated by exhortations with general addresses but introducing statements expressing consequences for specific categories (22: 31 f., 69: 37; cf. also 102: 25 c–29). For preceding alternatives cf. above.

2.5.2.3. Psalms 25: 22 and 28: 9 contain imperatives, directed to YHWH and expressing wishes concerning the people (cf. also the nominal clauses of 28: 8, and, on the same theme, 18: 51). For preceding alternatives cf. above.

2.5.3. Psalm 22 is concluded by כי עשה—similar constructions are found in Ps. 71: 19 a (עשית אשר) and 109: 27 (עשיתה) and seems to have a terminal function (cf. also Ps. 52: 11).

## 2.6. A summary of the above observations gives the following table:

| A | B | C | D | E | F | G |
|---|---|---|---|---|---|---|
| (ki and) perf 2/3sg | ki and impf 2/3sg | Modal impf 1sg | Modal impf 3pl (1sg) | ki and perf 1sg or nominal clauses | Modal impf 2/3sg with first person sing object | Other material |
| 9b, 10a | | | 11 | | | |
| | 6b | 15 | | | | |
| 20c | | 50 | | | | 47–49, 51 |
| 22b | | 23, 26 | | | | 24–25, 27, 28–29/30–32 |
| | 15b | | (20c), 21a | 20d, 21b | | 22 |
| | 12b | | | | | |
| 6b | | 7 | | | | 8, 9 |
| 12 | | 13 | | | | |
| 8c–9, 22 | | 8a–b | (18a), 18c–19 | 18b | | 23, 24, 25 |
| | | | (15–17) | | 18b (18d) | |
| 14a | | 13b | | | | |
| 6 | | 5, 9a | | | | 7–8 |
| | | 31 | 7 | 8a | 30b | 32/33–34 35–37 |
| | | 22, (23–24a) | 13 | | | 19a |
| 13b, 17c–d | 7b | 12 | 17b | | | |
| | | | | | | 25c–29 |
| | 31 | 30 | 28f | | | 27b, 31 |
| 7b, 8a | | 9 | | | | |
| | 13b | | | | | 14 |
| | 8d | | | | | |
| | | | | 12c | 10c–12b | |

3.1.1. The majority of the psalms which display concluding sections containing exhortations and (ki with) perf 2/3sg, combined with modal impfa 1sg or 3pl (6, 18: 2–7, 17–20, 28: 1–7, 30: 9–13, 31: 2–9, 61: 2–6 and 116: 1–9; cf. also 22: 2–23) show a common basic pattern, consisting of an introduction (not compulsory), and exhortations with motivations followed by one of the above mentioned alternative conclusions.

This pattern is enlarged at various points: in Pss. 18 and 116 the introductions are followed by accounts of misery (18: 5–6,[6] 116: 3 a–b) and descriptions of the invocational situation (18: 7 a–b, 116: 3 c–4 a; cf. also vv. 5–6 with hymnic traits), in Ps. 30 (v. 10) by questions, addressed to YHWH; in Ps. 6 the opening exhortations introduce a description of misery (vv. 7–8), in Ps. 31 expressions of confidence (vv. 6–7). It should be noted that these "enlargements" contain few instances of relevant formulaic language: Ps. 18: 5 a, 6 a, 6 b have their only counterpart in Ps. 116: 3 a, 3 b, Ps. 6: 8 a shows similarities to Ps. 31: 10 c, and Ps. 31: 7 a lacks comparative material within the starting group.

The initial exhortation of Ps. 22 (v. 12 a) is followed by a very detailed account of distress and misery (vv. 12 b–17, 18–19)—it is uncertain whether this account should be considered an enlargement of the basic pattern or an independent section; of two occurrences of formulaic language within the section (v. 12 a, 14 a), the first differs functionally from the other members of its group, and the second lacks relevant comparative material.

The structure of Ps. 143 shows similarities to the pattern, even though the conclusion differs from those mentioned above; the psalm opens with exhortations and motivations (vv. 1–4), followed by a section containing a review (vv. 5–6; the formulaic language of v. 5 a, 5 b and 5 c lacking comparative material within the starting group), further exhortations with motivations (vv. 7–10 b), and modal impfa with first person sing object, motivated by ki and a nominal clause.

Psalm 56 and parts of Ps. 86 do not conform to the pattern: in Ps. 56 the motivation of the first imperative has grown into a detailed description of a third party, interrupted by expressions of confidence (vv. 2 c–7, 9–12— v. 8 is obscure); Ps. 86 not only contains recurrent nominal clauses expressing confidence (cf. above n. F 3), but shows terminal traits in v. 7, 12–13 and 17 (cf. above 2.6; for Ps. 86: 1–8 cf. below 3.1.2)—the section 9–10 displays subject matter otherwise not known in the psalm and lacks first person sing references (and formulaic language); vv. 14–17 open with an account of distress followed by two nominal clauses (vv. 14–15; the formulaic language of v. 15 lacking comparative material within the starting group) and further by exhortations and modal impfa 3pl, motivated by ki and perf 2sg-s1sg (vv. 16–17)—this section may be regarded as a variant of the basic pattern.

3.1.2. The concluding alternative "ki and impf 2/3sg" presents a wide variety of form and function: ki with impf 2sg has first person sing suffixes in Ps. 17: 6, 86: 7, 142: 8, ki with impf 3sg shows first person sing object in Ps. 25: 15, third person sing in Ps. 140 (cf. also 3.1.3.1 for Ps. 109: 31). The preceding clauses are mainly verbal (cf. above 2.3)—only Ps. 25: 15 presents a nominal clause.

The structures of Ps. 17: 1–6 b, 25: 1–15, 86: 1–8, 140 and 142 vary considerably: in Ps. 17 the terminal section is preceded by exhortations with descriptions of a third party (vv. 1–2), followed by statements of blameless-ness (vv. 3–5); in Ps. 86 by exhortations with motivations (vv. 1–4), nomi-nal clauses expressing confidence (v. 5), and further exhortations introduc-ing a description of the invocational situation (vv. 6–7 a); in Ps. 140 by ex-hortations with qualifications (vv. 2–4, 5–6), followed by a transition (vv. 7–8) and further exhortations with qualifications (vv. 9–12); in Ps. 142 by an account of the invocational situation (vv. 2–4 b), followed by a de-scription of want (vv. 4 c–5), a transition (v. 6), and exhortations with motivations (vv. 7–8 a)—for Ps. 25: 1–15 cf. above 1.1.1.

No common basic pattern can be discerned in this group, nor do any of the psalms fit that described under 3.1.1.

3.1.3.1. Modal impfa 1sg not combined with other concluding alternatives are found in Ps. 17: 15 and 26: 12 (22: 26 will be treated below)—Ps. 71: 22 (23–24 a) and 109: 31, both with uncertain connexions in context, may also be included in this category.

Psalm 17: 6 c–15 and parts of Pss. 71 and 109 show certain structural simi-larities to the basic pattern isolated under 3.1.1: Ps. 17: 6 c–9 contain exhor-tations with qualifications—the latter grow into a detailed description of a third party (vv. 10–12, without formulaic language), followed by further exhortations with qualification (v. 13) and description (v. 14, without for-mulaic language). The concluding clauses in the cohortative (v. 15) lack the otherwise common connexion to perfa 2/3sg (cf. K 2.6).

Psalm 109 opens with exhortations introducing motivations and qualifica-tions (vv. 1–5), followed by wishes concerning a third party (vv. 6–20; the formulaic v. 15 b lacking comparative material within the starting group), exhortations with motivations, which develop into a description of personal misery (vv. 21–25), further exhortations introducing perf. 2sg (vv. 26–27), a section contrasting the activities of a third party and YHWH (vv. 28–29), without formulaic language), and finally modal impfa 1sg motivated by the somewhat surprising <u>ki</u> with impf 3sg and *third* person sing object (vv. 30, 31).

The sections 1–5, 21–25, 26–27, 28–29 and 30–31 describe a third party in plural categories, the former three also contain exhortations with first person sing object, while vv. 6–19 express wishes concerning a third party described in the singular—this may provide a provisional basis for distinction between two units. However, v. 20, initiated by a demonstrative pronoun, and forming the conclusion of vv. 6–19, contains two first person sing suffixes and points terminologically towards vv. 1–5 (and 28–29, 30–31): שטן in v. 20 a' is also found in v. 4 a (and 28 a), דבר in v. 20 b and 2 b; to רע of v. 20 b answers רעה of v. 5 a (cf. also נפש in v. 20 b and 31 b). A possible explanation of these phenomena would be that v. 20 is a transition, linking vv. 1–5 to v. 26 ff. (cf. below).

Another problem concerns the section 21–25: the account of misery (vv. 22–25, without relevant formulaic language) does not pick up the motifs from vv. 2–5, nor does the section share anything but the expression עני ואביון (v. 22 a) with vv. 6–19/20 (cf. v. 16 b).

If any compositional principle whatever underlies Ps. 109, it may be suggested that the sections 1–5, 26–27, and 28–29 belong together: the initial exhortation is followed by a motivating account of the activities of a plural category (vv. 1–5), renewed exhortations (v. 26) introduce the "Erkenntnisformel" of v. 27, and v. 28 picks up the third party from vv. 2–5 (and 27 a) and contrasts their activity with that of YHWH (mentioned in v. 27 b). Modal impfa 3pl conclude the unit (v. 29).

The remaining sections (v. 6–19/20, and 21–25) deviate from the basic pattern; vv. 30–31 provide the conclusion of the psalm in its present form.

In Ps. 26 the introductory summary (v. 1) is followed by exhortations (v. 2) with contents differing from those isolated under 1.3.1.1 and 1.3.2.1. The motivations of v. 3 develop into an account of blamelessness (vv. 4–8), followed by further exhortations and descriptions of a third party (vv. 9–10). v. 11 a underlines the blamelessness and introduces two imperatives (v. 11 b–c). The conclusion (v. 12) contains perf 3sg and (modal) impf 1sg. Ps. 26 does not conform to the basic pattern.

Under F 2.3.6 it was suggested that Ps. 71: 22 may be the conclusion of vv. 2–5, 9–11 and 12–13—if this is correct, the isolated unit contains exhortations with motivations (vv. 2–5), further exhortations with motivations (vv. 9–11), and exhortations introducing modal impfa 3pl and modal impfa 2sg (vv. 12–13, 22). With the exception of vv. 19 b–20 remaining sections of Ps. 71 could be read as a coherent unit with uniform terminology (cf. above n. F 38): vv. 6–8 expressing confidence, vv. 14–15/16–19 a containing proclamations of praise and confidence, and, finally, vv. 23–24 a on the same theme—this second unit does not conform to the pattern isolated under 3.1.1.

v. 1 is seen as the heading, v. 24 b as the conclusion of the psalm in its present form.

3.1.3.2. Modal impfa 1sg contextually combined with other material are found in Ps. 18: 50, 61: 9 and 69: 31.

Psalm 18: 50 is, through the initial ʿal ken, connected with a section presenting hymnic traits (vv. 47–49) and a terminology related to that of vv. 32–46: צור in v. 47 a and 32 b, נתן ··· האל in v. 48 a and 33, קמי in v. 49 b and 40 b—cf. also 48 b – 39, 40 and 49 a – 44 a.

vv. 31/32–49 bear no resemblance to the basic pattern, nor to any other units so far treated; vv. 21–25, 26–30/31 lack such introductory alternatives as reported under K 1, concluding alternatives discussed under K 2, and show only one example of formulaic language (vv. 31 b–c, lacking comparative material within the starting group)—thus these sections are of minor interest for this investigation.

Psalm 61: 2–6 conforms to the basic pattern: introduction, exhortation with motivations, and a conclusion consisting of modal impfa 1sg with ki and perfa 2sg. However, also v. 9 contains what has been designated "terminal traits". The stanza is conditional and dependent upon the modal impfa of vv. 7–8—this section displays subject matter not otherwise known from the psalm and lacks formulaic language. Smaller sections with the same motifs are also found in Ps. 18: 51 and 28: 8—both of them preceded by "regular" conclusions, and lacking formulaic language.

The compositional principles behind Ps. 69 are difficult to specify. However, three sections contain exhortations: vv. 2–6, 14–16 and 17–20. With the exception of "enemies" (v. 5) and "YHWH's knowledge" (v. 6), which are found in vv. 17–20, the motifs of vv. 2–6 recur in vv. 14–16. The sections 7–8/9–13 and 21–22 (lacking formulaic language) deal with disgrace and forsakenness; vv. 23–28 (lacking formulaic language) contain wishes concerning an unspecified third party.

Tentatively I suggest the following basic structure for Ps. 69: vv. 2–6, containing exhortations, motivations and an outline of distress, ending with ʾatta yadaʿtā, followed by vv. 14–16, with exhortations, initiated by waʾᵃni, vv. 17–20 with exhortations and motivations, ending with ʾatta yadaʿta, and finally a conclusion in vv. 30–31, initiated by waʾᵃni. The sections 7–8/9–13, 21–22 and 23–29 deviate from the basic pattern. vv. 32, 33–34, and 35–37 will be discussed below.

3.1.4.1. Modal impfa 3 pl (or neg impfa 1sg) combined with ki and perfa 1sg are found in Ps. 25: 20 c, 21 a, and in Ps. 31: 18 a, 18 c–d.

For Ps. 25: 1–15 cf. above 3.1.2. vv. 16–20 b contain exhortations with motivations, followed by neg impf 1sg, motivated by ki and perf 1sg (vv. 20 c–d). v. 21 (without formulaic language) opens with impfa 3pl, motivated by ki and perf 1sg. Even though this combination of concluding alternatives is unique, Ps. 25: 16–21 might be considered a variant of the basic pattern. v. 22 will be treated below.

The compositional principles behind Ps. 31 are difficult to specify: vv. 8–9, 18 a–b and 22 display terminal traits, vv. 2–9 and 15–18 b show a related terminology, while vv. 10–14 (with formulaic language only at the outset of the section), vv. 20–21, and 24–25 (both lacking relevant formulaic language) contain subject matter not known to the rest of the psalm—the former focuses on the problem of misery and forsakenness, the latter two deal with a third party with special relations to YHWH and lack first person sing references.

It was suggested above (F 2.1.2) that the section 15–18 b is a recapitulation, i.e. of the circumstances reported in vv. 2–9; vv. 18 c–19 are not included in this review since they are not terminologically related to vv. 2–9.

If vv. 2–9 and 15–18 b belong together, two of the concluding alternatives would be satisfactorily explained—however, vv. 22 and 23 still present a problem: preceded by a section with hymnic traits and plural objects, and followed by exhortations and qualifications addressed to a plural category, the stanzas stand isolated in context.

Several commentators have attracted attention to the break between v. 9 and v. 10—the section 10–14 bears little resemblance to the rest of the psalm but displays subject matter also found in the smaller units 69: 7–8/9–13 and 109: 21–25 (cf. also 22: 7–11, 12–17/18–19). I shall return to the composition of Ps. 31 (cf. 4.1.1).

3.1.4.2. Modal impfa 3pl combined with impf 2sg–s1sg are found in Ps. 40: 15–17, 18. The initial exhortations (v. 14) introduce wishes concerning two categories—those with a negative attitude to the psalmist, and those with a positive attitude to YHWH (vv. 15–17)—followed by a presentation of the psalmist, which leads up to impf 3pl, an expression of confidence, and a negative command. The unit presents similarities to the basic pattern, but the subsections are proportionally distorted and the conclusion is rare.

3.1.5. Psalm 143 is concluded by part pr n-s (v. 12 c), forming the motivation to the preceding modal impfa (vv. 10 c–12 b).

The psalm is initiated by exhortations with motivations (vv. 1–4 b), followed by a section with perfa 1sg (vv. 4 c–6—the formulaic language of vv. 5 a–b, 5 c lacking comparative material within the starting group). vv. 7–10 b contain exhortations with motivations.

The psalm conforms to the basic pattern—vv. 4 c–6 may be seen as an "enlargement".

3.1.6. Most of the material under K 2.6 has now been discussed. The remaining alternative conclusions were classified as "other material" above but could, according to content, be divided into sections dealing with "king/Messiah" (Ps. 18: 51, 28: 8, 61: 7–8), "patriotic" sections (25: 22, 28: 9, 69: 35–37, 109: 25 c–29), sections dealing with "subgroups" (22: 24–25, 27, 31: 24–25, 69: 33–34, 140: 14), and with "universalism" (22: 28–29/30–32). With the exception of Ps. 102: 25 c–29 these sections are preceded by other alternative conclusions.

3.1.6.1. The "king/Messiah"–motif is realized in Ps. 18: 51, 28: 8 and 61: 7–8. Gunkel (1926) comments on Ps. 28: 8, 61: 7f. (and 63: 12 a, 84: 9f., I S. 2: 10): "da sie gegenwärtig an falscher Stelle stehen, (sind sie) sicher spätere Zusätze, etwa eines seinem Herrscher besonders ergebenen Lesers, oder sie sind zu den ursprünglichen Gedichten hinzugekommen, als diese im Königstempel, jedenfalls von Jerusalem, aufgeführt worden sind." The king "kann nichts anderes als der König Israels oder Judas sein. ... (es handelt sich hier) um den *regierenden König*". There is no reason to contradict this general reference to the time of the monarchies as far as Ps. 28: 8 and 61: 7–8 are concerned—great caution should however be observed with regard to evaluation and dating of Ps. 18: 51, as Ps. 18 in its present form seems to be a combination of different literary units.

3.1.6.2. The "patriotic" sections may be subdivided into shorter units, containing exhortations, addressed to YHWH, followed by a specification of the object (Ps. 25: 22, 28: 9),[7] and such presenting "hymnic" phraseology with creation motifs, introducing statements concerning plural categories. (Ps. 69: 35–37, 102: 25 c–29—cf. also 102: 13/14–23). In the first group the exhortations mainly deal with "saving" and the objects are "Israel", "your people" or "your heritage"; the second group speaks of "the sons of your servants", "their offspring", "the offspring of his servants" and "those who love his name" in connexion with the verbs שכן, נחל, ישב, ירש.

Apart from vv. 25 c–29, Ps. 102 lacks sections with terminal traits; the psalm opens with exhortations and motivations (vv. 2–4), introducing a description of distress (vv. 5–12, without formulaic language). The "hymnic" v. 13 forms a system together with Lm. 5: 19; vv. 14–23 (without formulaic language) lack first person sing references and deal with the relation YHWH – Zion – the peoples.

The perfa 3sg of v. 24 do not necessarily refer to YHWH—the stanza may be a continuation of the account of personal distress (cf. ימי in v. 4 a,

12 a and 24 b); vv. 25 a–b, containing a negative command, address YHWH, and are directly followed by a section with creation motifs and statements concerning plural categories (25 c–29)—this conclusion is not only unusual but seems somewhat abrupt.[8]

J. Becker (1966: 44 f.) considers vv. 2–12 as an originally independent "individual lament" of which vv. 24–25 b may also have been a part. This lament was subject to rereading or "Neuinterpretation" during exilic or post-exilic times (24 ff.)—vv. 13–23, 25 c–29 show the results of this interpretation. These sections "haben die Lage des Volkes im Exil und die Heimkehr zum Sion vor Augen. Die Exilierten werden, ‚der Ausgeplünderte' (v. 18), ‚der Gefangene' und ‚Söhne des Todes' (v. 21) genannt. Gedanken und Sprache lehnen sich anerkanntermassen stark an deutero- und tritoisaianische Texte an, die ja auch aus derselben heilsgeschichtlichen Situation geschrieben sind."[9] The interpretations show eschatological traits; the return from the Exile and the confrontation (*Auseinandersetzung*) with the nations in considered the outset of a new era.

From the sections 102: 13–23, 25 c–29 Becker has combined the main ideas of exilic/post-exilic rereading of "individual laments":[10]

1. die Herrschaft des auf ewig thronenden Gottes Israels, der in der Schöpfung seine Macht erweist.
2. die Offenbarung seiner Herrschaft auf dem wiederhergestellten Sion nach der Heimkehr des Volkes aus dem Exil.
3. die Anerkennung Jahwes durch die Völker, die sich am Sion versammeln.
4. der Hinweis auf spätere Generationen, denen das Land und die Segnungen Jahwes einmal zuteil werden sollen.

These main ideas are not only found in parts of Ps. 102—Ps. 69 too contains thematically related sections: v. 35 corresponds to number one above,[11] v. 36 to number two, and v. 37 to number four.[12]

Becker includes v. 33 in the "original" psalm but has problems with v. 34—the stanza could be seen as a reference to persons in the same situation as the (original) psalmist or as a piece of redactional work (46 f.). Now, if v. 34 belongs to the original material, the redactor must have given the categories mentioned in vv. 33–34 a new interpretation—as opposed to the ʿ<u>a</u>nawim etc., of the individual thanksgivings (the example offered is Ps. 22: 27), they come to stand for "die frommen Israeliten" in general (47).

It is, however, somewhat difficult to see the need for two different interpretations of Ps. 22: 24–25, 27 and 69: 33–34:

כי שמע אל אביונים יהוה　　יראי יהוה הללוהו
ואת אסיריו לא בזה　　כל זרע יעקב כבדוהו
ראו ענוים וישמחו　　וגורו ממנו כל זרע ישראל
דרשי אלהים ויחי לבבכם　　כי לא בזה ולא שקץ ענות עני
ולא השתיר פניו ממנו
ובשועו אליו שמע
יאכלו ענוים וישבעו
יהללו יהוה דרשיו
יחי לבבכם לעד

The ki-clauses of Ps. 22:25 form the motivations to exhortations addressed to plural categories; the ki-clauses of Ps. 69:34 might also be seen as motivations for the preceding clauses (cf. above n. F 7); terminological similarities are present between 22:27–69:33 and 22:25–69:34 even though the objects of 22:25 are singular while those of 69:34 are plural. The conclusion is that Ps. 22:24–25, 27 and 69:33–34 could be ascribed a common "Horizont", so that if 69:33–34 deal with, or have been interpreted as dealing with "die frommen Israeliten" this is also true for Ps. 22:24–25, 27. Whether or not these sections are actually redactional will be considered below (3.1.6.3.).

In Ps. 22 Becker finds examples of rereading in vv. 28–32[13] even though direct references to exilic phenomena are lacking. However, through Is. 44:23, the concluding ki'asa is given a "heilsgeschichtlich–eschatologische" interpretation and seen as a link with Pss. 69 and 102: "Das in Is. 44, 23 und in Ps. 69, 35 nur in kosmischen Jubel angedeutete Königtum Jahwes wird ausdrücklich erwähnt in Ps. 102, 13 und 22, 29." Furthermore, motif one above is present in v. 29, motif three in vv. 28–30 b even though Zion is not mentioned, motif four in vv. 30 c–32[14] (cf. also Is. 61:9, 65:9 and 53:10).[15]

Summing up: originally cultic units (individual laments and thanksgivings) have been disengaged from their original "Sitz im Leben" and, through exilic or post-exilic "Neuinterpretation", applied to a new situation—a situation considered as the outset of a new era.

The sections: 22:28–30, 31–32, 69:35–37 and 109:13–23 25 c–29 are of particular interest to the present author, even though there is some confusion as to the exact limitations of the "original" material in these units.

3.1.6.3. The sections dealing with "subgroups" contain imperatives (2m plur) (Ps. 22:24, 31:24/25) or modal impfa (3pl) (22:27, 69:33, 140:14).

The imperatives (2m plur) are the following: כבד הלל גור, אהב[III], with YHWH as object—Ps. 31:25 has the unrelated חזק; those addressed are "you who fear YHWH", "entire race of Jacob/Israel", "you devout", and "you who hope"; the motivations show perf 3sg with singular object in Ps. 22:25, nominal clauses with plural objects in Ps. 31:24.

Ps. 22:27 and 69:33 are commonly understood as belonging to preceding "thanksgivings" (so Gunkel, 1926:*ad* 22:27). Another interpretation is possible however: in the two stanzas the impfa appear in series (אכל-שבע הלל-חיה in 22:27, ראה-שמח-חיה in 69:33)—the combination אכל-שבע with the second member negated is represented in prophetic oracles of doom (Is. 9:19, Ho. 4:10, Mi. 6:14—cf. also Lv. 26:6), while אכל-שבע-הלל is found only in Jo. 2:26; (cf. also Dt. 8:10); the combination ראה-שמח is, in addition to Ps. 69:33, also found in Ps. 107:42 and Jb. 22:19. Jb. 22:15–20 seems to be a collection of various quotations, while Ps. 107:33–43 and Jo. 2:19–27 deal with restoration. Discussing Ps. 107:33–43 H.-J. Kraus observes: "Sowohl in der inhaltlichen Aussagetendenz wie auch in Einzelheiten ist ein Zusammenhang zur Verkündigung Deuterojesajas (Jes. 40–55) zu erkennen" (1960:*ad loc.*); concerning Jo. 2:26a (conscious) adaptation of earlier oracles is feasible—in the new situation the aspect of doom is however changed into a promise by the omission of the negative and the addition of הלל.

If this interpretation is correct, Ps. 22:27 and 69:33–34 would be further examples of exilic/post-exilic "Neuinterpretation"—this would also be true of 22:24–25, since this section was ascribed the same "Horizont" as the other two (cf. above 3.1.6.2). v. 26 contains references to first person sing, but should be included in the larger section 24–27, which constitutes a comment on, and application of, vv. 22b–23; the אחים and קהל are interpreted as יראי יהוה, זרע יעקב/ישראל (v. 24) and are, in turn, invited to praise YHWH (הלל cf. also v. 23b, 27b) and to honor and fear him, with motivations referring to his intervention (cf. v. 22b). The contents of v. 23 are reformulated in v. 26 with two notable terminological differences: the אחים are now יראים (cf. v. 24a) and the קהל is a קהל רב (cf. also Ps. 35:18, 40:10f., Ez. 10:1)—for v. 27 cf. above. Thus from what is formally an account of individual salvation the perspective is widened in that this salvation comes to provide a basis of hopefulness for several.

3.1.6.4. The sections dealing with "universalism" included Ps. 22:28–29/30–32 and 86:9–10. I pointed out above that Ps. 22:24–27 may be seen as an application of the salvation accounted for in v. 22b, and that vv. 28–32 have been regarded as an example of exilic/post-exilic "Neuinterpretation"—the relation between the two remains to be investigated however.

The זכר (abs) of v. 28 is strange at the outset of an independent section, but could be explained on the basis of vv. 24–27. The categories mentioned in v. 28 are no longer national but universal, the motivations of v. 29 no longer pertain to isolated saving activity but to the sovereignty of YHWH. Thus a continued widening of perspective can be observed.

The אכלו of v. 30a has caused great problems among the commentators, but could perhaps be explained against the background of v. 27 (and 28)—if so, an account of individual salvation is applied both to national subgroups and the nations.

For Ps. 86:9–10 cf. below 3.2.1.3.

3.1.6.5. No comment has so far been made on Ps. 25:22, 28:9, 31:24(–25) and 140:14; the former two were labelled "patriotic", the latter deal with "subgroups". Ps. 25:22 breaks the acrostic pattern and uses אלהים instead of the יהוה of vv. 1–21, but no criteria for diachronic reasoning are present within the stanza—this is also true for Ps. 28:9.

Ps. 31:24(–25) and 140:14 refer to צדיקים, חסים, אמונים, (עשה גאוה), and ישרים but display contents too general to provide a basis for diachronic speculations.

3.2. Within the psalms there are sections similar in form and/or contents to the units dealt with under K 3.1.6.1–5 and likewise devoid of relevant formulaic language, i.e. Ps. 31:20–21, 71:19b–20, 86:9–10 and 116:5–6. For Ps. 102:13–23 cf. above 3.1.6.2.

3.2.1.1. Psalm 31:20–21 shows hymnic traits and contains plural objects; those mentioned are יראים and חסים, and the divine activity is described as טוב in terms of צפן, פעל and סתר. Of these טוב is very often associated with possession of the Land (Ho. 3:5, Jr. 2:7, 31:12, 14, Ezr. 9:25, Ne. 9:25, 35 ff.) and פעל with YHWH's creative and saving activity (Ex. 15:7, Nb. 23:22–23, Is. 26:12, 41:4, Ps. 44:2, 68:9), while the others show rather wide areas of application.

The form and content of Ps. 31:20–21 were considered too general to indicate a distinctive "Horizont"—this was also true of v. 24 (25) (cf. 3.1.6.5); furthermore, the section forms part of a cluster of units (vv. 18b–19, 20–21, 22, 23, 24, 25) with unclear interrelations and indeterminate dependence upon vv. 2c–9, 15–18b.

3.2.1.2. Psalm 71:19b–20 shows hymnic traits and contains first person plural objects.[16] The terminology is similar to that of Ps. 30:4: חיה and עלה with prep and noun signifying the "nether world" (for this import of תהום cf. Ez. 26:19f., Jon. 2:6f.)—further comments on the collocation will be given below (4.1.2).

Psalm 86: 9–10 contains motifs similar to those of Ps. 22: 28–29/30–32: the nations (86: 9 a, 22: 28 b) will/should bow down (86: 9 b, 22: 28 b, 30 b) before the Almighty (86: 10 b, 22: 29).

3.2.1.3. Psalm 116: 5–6 shows hymnic traits; vv. 5–6 a contain plural references, while vv. 6 b–c have perf 1sg–impf 3sg with first person sing object. The terminology of the section is unusual: מרחם as a divine epithet is used only in v. 5 and in Is. 49: 10, 54: 10, פתאים without contrasting noun outside Pr. only in Ez. 45: 20, Ps. 9: 8 and 119: 130, דלל in v. 6 and Ps. 142: 7 (sing) and 79: 8 (plur). The divine name of v. 5 is the only instance of אלהים within the psalm, and the suffix is the only plural one.

These observations might be taken as indicating a separate origin of vv. 5–6—the section would then offer a ("misplaced") example of collective application of an account of individual salvation, but the criteria are too vague for a diachronic evaluation of Ps. 116: 5–6.

4. Psalms 6, 18: 2–7+17–20, 28: 1–7, 30: 9–13, 31: 2–9, 61: 2–6, 116: 1–9 and 143 conform to a common basic pattern, Ps. 17: 6 c–15, 25: 16–21, 71: 2–5, 9–13, 22 and 86: 14–17 show similarities to this pattern (cf. also 69: 2–6, 14–20, 30–31 and 109: 1–5, 26–27, 30, and 22: 2–23). In the search for a common Gattung, constituting or reflecting a ritual, my next step will be to investigate the frequency of relevant formulaic language within these units (cf. above C and J 2.1.4).

4.1.1. Psalms 6, 18: 2–7+17–20, 28: 1–7, 31: 2–9, 71: 2–5, 9–13, 22, 116: 1–9 and 143 contain a high amount of relevant formulaic language; those sections which lack, or show very few instances of such language mainly coincide with the passages designated "enlargements" above, or form part of introductions (Ps. 6: 7–8, 18: 2–4, 31: 6–7, 116: 1–2, 143: 1–4 b, 4 c–6). With the exception of Pss. 18 and 116, where accounts of misery precede the exhortations, the aforesaid units belong to the first of the two main categories isolated under 1.3.

Lord (1974: 43) states: "The phrases for the ideas most commonly used become more securely fixed than those for less frequent ideas"—as observed above, the most common formulas/formulaic systems contain exhortations, short motivations and pledges, while more substantial references to enemies or personal distress tend to be non-formulaic. Thus it may be suggested that there existed a convention for the composition of "individual laments" with exhortations, short motivations and pledges securely fixed, while prolonged motivations could be moulded to fit special situations.

In two instances supplements with related terminology follow upon the "lament" proper: Ps. 116: 10–17 states the personal consequences of salvation (cf. above n. F 9), Ps. 31: 15–18 b contains a summary of vv. 2 c–9 (cf. F 2.1.2). Ps. 31: 2 c–9 and 15–18 b frame a section (vv. 10–14), thematically focusing on misery and forsakenness, and containing formulaic language only at the outset. In terms of structure and content this section differs from vv. 2–9, 15–18 b and a "Horizont" deviating from the main part of the psalm may tentatively be suggested (cf. 3.1.4.1). As the sections 18 c–19, 20–21, 22, 23, 24/25 also show loose connexions to vv. 2–9 and 15–18 b, and unclear interrelations, one is inclined to agree with Kittel (1922: *ad loc.*) who judges the psalm as a "... nach vorhandenen Texten zusammengestelltes Gebet".

In Ps. 18 the "lament" has been combined with units containing very few instances of formulaic language (cf. J 1.3), and showing motifs and terminology differing from vv. 5–7+17–20 (vv. 21–25/26–30/31, 31/32–46/47–50, 51)—certain expressions recur however: צור in v. 3, 32, 47, ישעי in v. 3, 47, 51, דרך in v. 22, 31, 33, תמים in v. 24, 26, 31, 33 (for vv. 47–50 cf. above n. F 59 and 3.1.3.2). Concerning motifs and terminology vv. 8–16 differ from the "lament" proper, and the five instances of formulaic language point towards a "Horizont" other than that of the main group.

In Ps. 71 the "lament" was thought to comprise the sections 2–5, 9–11, 12–13 and 22 (cf. 3.1.3.1), while vv. 6–8, 14–19 a and 23–24 a (lacking relevant formulaic language) may be read as a separate unit with recurrent terminology (cf. above n. F 38). In combining the two units the principle seems to have been thematical—both cover a period "from youth to old age" (cf. אל תעזבני in v. 9, 18, מנעורי in v. 5, 17, זקנה in v. 9, 18). v. 1 is seen as the introduction to the psalm in its present form, v. 24 b as the conclusion; vv. 19 b–20 (cf. 3.2.1.2) and 21 might be considered redactional transitions. The vocabulary of v. 21 is uncommon: for רבה cf. Jb. 10: 17 (with cop.), for סבב impf 2sg Ps. 114: 5, for רחם impf 2sg Pi'el Ps. 119: 182 and Is. 12: 1 (with cop.), for גדלה 2 S. 7: 21, 23, Ps. 145: 3, 6, Est. 1: 4, 6: 3, 10: 2, 1 Ch. 17: 19, 21, and 29: 11.

For Ps. 28: 8, 9 cf. 3.1.5.1, 2.

4.1.2.1. Psalm 30: 9–13 conforms to the basic pattern but shows only one instance of relevant formulaic language; conformity with the pattern points towards a *time* of origin when compositional conventions are vivid, whereas a low amount of formulaic language indicates a *situation* different from that of the "formulaic psalms". The relationship between the "lament" and vv. 2–4/5–6 however deserves to be investigated, as the formulaic language of v. 5 points towards a special group of psalms (for v. 5 a cf. Ps. 98: 5 a, for 5 b 97: 12 b).[17]

vv. 2–4/5–6 and 9–13 show certain terminological similarities (cf. v. 4 and 10, 5 and 13)—there are, however, differences in the application of the conceptions: vv. 2–4 underline the saving activity, v. 10 poses questions, v. 5 contains plural exhortations and is followed by motivations without first person references, v. 13 is dependent upon the preceding perfa 2sg with first person objects. Within vv. 2–4 the statements about salvation appear to pertain to an individual (cf. vv. 9–13)—a closer scrutiny points however in another direction: Of 16 instances of רפא (Qal) c. acc, 12 deal with "healing" of the *people* (Is. 57: 18f., Jr. 30: 17, 33: 6, Ho. 6: 1, 11: 3, Ps. 60: 4, 107: 20, 2 Ch. 7: 14, 30: 20; Is. 30: 26, Jr. 3: 22 and Ho. 14: 5), who, having turned away from apostacy and sin, will be *restored;* עלה (Hiph.) followed by prep and noun signifying "grave" or "nether world" is found only in Jon. 2: 7 and Ez. 37: 12, 13—the latter two in connexion with national re-establishment and life (Ez. 37: 14; cf. Ps. 30: 4 b).

Thus, against a background dealing with salvation, and applying prophetic terminology originally pertaining to the restoration of Israel, a plural category is summoned to praise YHWH—this is to be compared with the above observations on Ps. 22: 24ff. and 69: 33 ff.

In the "lament" proper, v. 10 (cf. also Ps. 6: 6, 88: 11, Is. 38: 18) lacks references to "saving" and "life" and applies a terminology common in references to literal, individual dying/death (cf. Gen. 37: 35, Nb. 16: 30, 33, Ez. 32: 27, Ps. 55: 12, Jb. 7: 9, 33: 24, Is. 38: 18, *et al.*). The actual situation of the psalmist is not described in vv. 9–13, while v. 2 mentions "enemies"; the salvation is only implied in the "lament", as against the references to "healing" and "revival" in vv. 3–4. This leads to the supposition that vv. 9–13 and 2–6 have been combined so that the "salvation" of an individual is taken as presaging the "salvation" of the nation. vv. 7–8 may be seen as a redactional transition.

4.1.2.2. Psalm 61: 2–6 conforms to the basic pattern; it is however unusual that the combination modal impf (v.3)–motivating ki-clauses (4)–cohortatives (5) is followed by additional ki-clauses. Furthermore, the motivations of v. 6 refer to the "promises" of the psalmist, to plural categories otherwise not known to vv. 2–6, and the terminology is unusual: Outside Ps. 61: 6 שמע לנדר is only found in Nb. 30: 5 in another type of context and without preposition, ירשה without references to distribution of territory in context, only in Jr. 32: 8.

The section 7–9 might be considered "spätere Zusätze" (cf. 3.1.6.1). This section contains the fairly common expression שלם נדר (v. 9 b, cf. also 2 S. 15: 7, Is. 19: 21, Ps. 22: 26, 50: 4, 65: 2, 66: 13, 116: 14, 18, Pr. 7: 14, Jb. 22: 27), which may explain שמע לנדרי of v. 6 a—i.e. if v. 6 is con-

sidered a redactional transition, picking up שמע from the introduction of
vv. 2–5 and נדר from the conclusion of the additional section.

If this supposition is correct, and if ירשה has the same connotations as
in Dt. 2: 5, 9, 12, 19, 3: 20, Jos. 1: 15, 12: 6, 7, Jg. 21: 17 and 2 Ch. 20: 11,
Ps. 61: 6–9 would offer a combination of motifs similar to that of Ps. 28: 8.

Of the five instances of formulaic language in Ps. 61: 2–5/6 only two, i.e.
v. 2 a and 3 a, were considered relevant. v. 2 a was collated with Ps. 86: 6 a,
v. 3 a with Ps. 30: 9 and 28: 1 a; the comparison with Ps. 86: 6 and 30: 9 is
however questionable, since Ps. 86: 1–13 differs from the basic pattern and
Ps. 30: 9–13 contains only one example of formulaic language.

Thus, Ps. 61: 2–5/6 would point towards a *time* with vivid compositional
conventions, but indicate a *situation* differing from that of the "formulaic
psalms".

4.2.1. Psalms 17: 6 c–15, 25: 16–21 and 86: 14–17 bear some resemblance to
the basic pattern but contain very few examples of relevant formulaic
language (cf. J 1.2, 1.5, 1.15; for Ps. 71: 2–5, 9–13 and 22 cf. 4.1.1).

Similarities only to the basic pattern coupled with few elements of formulaic language do not demonstrate adherence to a compositional conven-
tion/tradition, but indicate a time and a situation where such a convention
is either not yet developed or no longer relevant. Thus, in the search for a
basic Gattung, constituting or reflecting a ritual, Ps. 17: 6 c–15, 25: 16–21
and 86: 14–17 are of minor interest.

4.2.2. Parts of Pss. 69 and 109 show similarities to the basic pattern—the
compositional principles behind these psalms are difficult to specify, and the
isolation of the units 69: 2–6, 14–20, 30–31 and 109: 1–5, 26–27, 30 must be
considered somewhat arbitrary (cf. 3.1.3.2 and 3.1.3.1).

The relevant formulaic language of Ps. 69 is concentrated to the section
17–20, containing exhortations with motivations and presenting fairly
general contents.

The conventional invocational language of the section 17–20 could be
regarded as the kernel of Ps. 69—a kernel which has been combined with
other invocational material, realized in a specific, non-conventional
language and thus indicating a specific situation. Due to the lack of relevant
comparative material the psalm cannot be said to constitute a realization of
a defined Gattung.

Psalm 109: 1–5, 26–27, 30 contains only one example of relevant formulaic
language, i.e. v. 26 b, which was collated with Ps. 6: 5 c. Abstracted similarities to the basic pattern and a few elements of formulaic language indicate
a time and a situation in which a compositional convention is not yet

developed or no longer relevant—thus Ps. 109 cannot be offered as an example of such a convention.

4.2.3. Psalm 22: 2–23 shows similarities to the basic pattern (for vv. 24–32 cf. 3.1.6.2–4) but contains an extended introduction (vv. 2–11) and a very detailed description of misery (vv. 12–17/18–19). The relevant formulaic language of Ps. 22 is concentrated to the section 20–23, containing exhortations and promises. This section might be seen as the kernel of Ps. 22—a kernel which has been combined with other invocational material, expressed in a specific, non-conventional language and thus indicating a specific situation. Due to the lack of relevant comparative material Ps. 22 cannot be said to constitute the realization of a defined Gattung.

5. Summing up: from Pss. 6, 18: 2–7, 17–20, 28: 1–7, 30: 1–13, 31: 2–9, 61: 2–6, 116: 1–9 and 143 a basic pattern, consisting of an introduction (not compulsory), exhortations with motivations and one, or a combination of, the concluding alternatives listed under 2.6, was inferred. This pattern could be enlarged at various points—thus the motivations in particular might be prolonged.

Applying Lord's observation that "the phrases for the ideas most commonly used become more securely fixed than those for less frequent ideas" (1974: 43), a convention for the composition of "individual laments" with exhortations, short motivations and pledges securely fixed, i.e. realized in formulaic language, was suggested. The prolonged motivations, mainly lacking such set language, were thought to have been moulded to fit special situations.

Ps. 6, 18: 2–7, 17–20, 28: 1–7, 31: 2–9, 71: 2–5, 9–13, 22, 116: 1–9 and 143 were offered as examples of such a compositional convention; these units conformed to the basic pattern and showed a stable formulaic language. It was also observed that the "laments" proper of Pss. 18, 28 and 71 have been combined with other material, showing differing contents and few occurrences of formulaic language, while Ps. 31: 15–18 b and 116: 10–19 contain applications of preceding themes. The combining principle seems to have been chiefly catenary.

As examples of units belonging in a time with a vivid compositional convention/tradition, but indicating specific situations, Ps. 30: 9–13 and 61: 2–5/6 were offered—these mainly conformed to the basic pattern but showed very few elements of formulaic language. Ps. 61: 2–5/6 was combined with a section, containing wishes concerning the king, Ps. 30: 9–13 preceded by a plural application of the themes from the "lament" proper.

As examples of units belonging in a time and a situation in which a compositional tradition was not yet developed or no longer relevant Ps. 17: 6 c–15, 25: 16–21, 86: 14–17 and 109 were offered; these units revealed only vague similarities to the basic pattern and presented very few elements of relevant formulaic language, while Ps. 22: 2–23 and 69 contained a kernel of set phrases and showed partial similarities to the basic pattern. Ps. 102 too has a kernel of formulaic language, i.e. the introductory section (vv. 2–4) displaying exhortations with motivations, the last of which introduces a detailed description of distress (vv. 5–12; for vv. 13–23, 25 c–29 cf. 3.1.6.2).

Ps. 17: 1–6 b, 25: 1–15, 26, 56, 86: 1–8/9–13, 140 and 142 did not conform to the basic pattern—of these Pss. 17, 25, 26, 56, 140 and 142 presented few elements of relevant formulaic language (cf. J 2.1.4).

The sections 1–5, 6–7 and 11–13 of Ps. 86 contained an unusual density of set phrases with references to units both within the main stream of tradition and to compositions mainly uninfluenced by compositional convention; the section 9–10 lacked formulaic language, but displayed subject matter similar to Ps. 22: 28–29/30–32. Two of the structuring stanzas of Ps. 86 contain first person sing references, i.e. v. 13 and v. 17 d—these two are also seen as the conclusions of preceding units, while v. 6 has third person plur object, and v. 8 and 10 show universalistic traits. Ps. 86 is the only example within the starting group of a formulaic psalm deviating from the basic pattern. It is difficult to specify the time and situation of the psalm, but the contents of vv. 8 and 9–10 indicate an exilic/post-exilic date for the unit in its present form.

Psalm 88 deviates from the basic pattern in that descriptions of invocational situation, containing perfa 1sg of *verba cordis*, appear thrice (vv. 2, 10 b–c and 14), detailed accounts of misery and distress twice (vv. 4/5–10 a, 16–19), and in the lack of conclusion. The psalm displays a low amount of relevant formulaic language.[18]

Psalms 22: 28–29/30–32, 69: 33–37 and 102: 13/14–23, 25 c–29, lacking relevant formulaic language, contain plural references and motifs also found in Is. 40–66. According to J. Becker (1966) these sections are the result of redactional activity in exilic or post-exilic times. Becker stresses that "Die Exilsituation und die sie fortführende nachexilische Heilserwartung ist ganz allgemein im Hinblick auf die Entstehung des Alten Testaments die entscheidende Zeit, die aus Traditionen und Quellen die Bücher der Schrift werden lässt. Hier ist der Standort fast aller alttestamentlichen Bücher, von dem aus sie—und wir mit ihnen—den Blick in die Vergangenheit Israels richten." After mentioning the Deuteronomist's and the Chronicler's works of history, the final redaction of the Pentateuch, and traces of redactional activity in the prophetic material he continues: "Eine Bewegung solchen

Ausmasses, die als restaurative Bewegung die Vergangenheit auffing, sie aber zugleich im Bewusstsein des neuen Heilswillen Jahwes neu deutete, konnte auch an den Psalmen nicht vorübergehen. Eine Reihe von Psalmen sind offenkundig in dieser Situation entstanden, andere, die als geprägte Form bereits bestanden, wurden durch redaktionelle Neuinterpretation in den Dienst der neuen Botschaft gestellt"(24 f.).

It has also been noticed that accounts of individual salvation have been applied to wider categories; so Ps. 22: 22 b–23, 30: 9–13 and 69: 30 b–31 provide backgrounds for summons addressed to (national) subgroups. With the exception of Ps. 30: 3, which was collated with Ps. 28: 1 a and 61: 3 a, Ps. 22: 24–27, 30: 2–6, 69: 33–34 lacked relevant formulaic language; the motifs and terminology of these sections suggested a setting similar to that of Ps. 22: 28–29/30–32, 69: 35–37 and 102: 13/14–23, 25 c–29, while the sections with references to subgroups or universal categories in Ps. 25: 22, 28: 9, 31: 20–21, 24(25), 86: 9–10, 116: 5–6) (lacking formulaic language) were considered too general to provide criteria for diachronic reasoning.

Of the psalms with traces of exilic/post-exilic activity Pss. 22, 69 and 102 only partially conformed to the basic pattern and showed formulaic language concentrated to sections containing general exhortations with motivations, while their main parts indicated special situations. Further study of particular motifs must precede a closer definition of these situations.

# L. IN SEARCH FOR AN
# "EBED YHWH"-COMPLEX

As stated in the premises the isolation of formal, linguistic elements means the location of specific contents; furthermore, the use of set phrases is probably not arbitrary but points back to a specific sphere of thought. The analysis of such phrases and their contents might therefore provide a basis for the isolation of the constituents of a cultural background of the psalms, and of "Schemata" within that background.

If there exists a number of "Ebed YHWH"-psalms, constituting or reflecting a ritual, these units would, according to my premises, belong to a common "Gattung", and should thus be sought among the psalms which conform to the compositional convention/tradition—the structure of the psalms would indicate the general structure of the ritual, the contents would reflect its main content. Having outlined the general structure and main locutionary elements of psalms conforming to the compositional convention, my next step is an attempt to isolate themes or motifs[1] characteristic of a presumptive "Ebed YHWH"-complex. However, aware of the possibility that such a closed group, constituting or reflecting a ritual, does *not* exist, I shall retain all the psalms from the starting group within the scope of the investigation, and thus make room for units which may present themes/motifs akin to those found in the Servant Songs of Deutero-Isaiah[2] without conforming to the compositional convention; similarities of theme/motif to units outside the starting group will also be noted (cf. below M 1).

1. Ps. 6, 18: (2–4), 5–7, 17–20, 28: (1–2), 3–7, 31: 2c–9, 71: 2–5, 9–13, 22, 116: (1–2), 3–9 and 143 contain substantial proportions of common formulaic language and conform basically to a common pattern. Exhortations with short motivations, followed by one or a number of the alternative conclusions isolated under K 2.6 show set language, while introductions in the form of summaries, reviews or outlines of the invocational situation, and slightly prolonged motivations contain few elements of formulaic language. The prolonged motivations were thought to have been moulded to fit specific situations, and thus not seen as realizations of a compositional convention, nor do the introductions adhere to such a convention, since they are related only to the units which they initiate.

With the exception of Ps. 18: 2–7, 17–20 and 116: 1–9, where formulaic descriptions of distress precede the exhortations, the units which conform to the compositional convention contain opening sections belonging to the first of the two groups isolated under K 1.3, while the conclusions vary, although, with the exception of Pss. 71 and 143, containing (ki and) perfa 2/3sg.

In the sections with exhortations and motivations, the most frequent summons to YHWH enjoin Him to "save" (Ps. 6: 5, 18: 17, 18, 20, 31: 2, 3, 71: 2, 4, 116: 4, and within psalms, 143: 9), and to "listen" (Ps. 31: 3, 71: 2, 143: 1—cf. also 143: 7)—for other exhortations within the group cf. K 1.3.1.1. The motivations contain expressions of confidence (Ps. 31: 4, 5, 71: 3, 5, 143: 10), references to the character or attributes of YHWH (Ps. 6: 5, 31: 4—for 116: 5–6 cf. K 3.2.1.3), and short accounts of the situation of the psalmist—a situation where "I have no strength left" (Ps. 6: 3), "my bones are in torment" (Ps. 6: 3), "my soul (is) in utter torment" (Ps. 6: 4), ". . . a foe too strong for me / they assail(ed) me on the day of my disaster" (Ps. 18: 18 b–19 a), "an enemy who hounds me to crush me in the dust, forces me to dwell in the darkness like the dead long ago / my spirit fails me and my heart is full of disaster" (Ps. 143: 3 f.), "my spirit fails —I shall go down to the Pit like the rest" (Ps. 143: 7)—additional references to "death" are found in Ps. 6: 6 and 116: 8, to a "hostile third party" in Ps. 6: 9, 11, 28: 3 ff., 31: 9, 71: 4, 10, 13 and 143: 9, 12, while Ps. 18: 18 mentions "great waters" (cf. also Ps. 18: 5–6, 116: 3, Jon. 2: 4 b–c, 6–7 b).

The concluding perfa 2/3sg speak of YHWH's having "heard" (Ps. 6: 9, 10, 28: 6), "rescued" (Ps. 116: 8), and "seen/known/not handed over/given space" (Ps. 31: 8 f.).

With the exception of Ps. 18: 17, which is apparently influenced by vv. 5–6, the terminology of the exhortations is too general to provide criteria for the isolation of themes/motifs characteristic of any specific category of "individual laments". Moreover, the motivations containing expressions of confidence, or referring to the character or attributes of YHWH present motifs not restricted to any special group of psalms—the brief descriptions of personal misery or distress and references to certain obstacles, however, may be expected to explain special situations, and thus deserve closer attention.

1.1. Ps. 6: 3 b speaks of "lack of strength" in an unusual terminology (cf. Neh. 3: 34), while the subsequent motivations (vv. 3 d–4) are rather stereotyped (for "afflicted bones" cf. Ps. 22: 15, 18, 31: 11, 102: 4, 6, within the starting group—cf. also Ps. 32: 3, 38: 4, 42: 11, 141: 7, Is. 38: 13, Jr. 23: 9, Hab. 3: 16, Jb. 19: 20, 30: 3, 17, 33: 19, Lm. 3: 4, 4: 8). No clue to the origin of these general afflictions is given in the section 2–6, nor does the "enlargement" of vv. 7–8 describe specific obstacles (for אנחה cf. Ps. 31:11, 102:6 within the starting group—cf. also Ps. 38:10, Jr. 45:3, Jb. 3:24, 23:2, Lm. 1:22).

Thus, from the account of personal misery in Ps. 6:2–6/7–8 no conclusions can be drawn as to the specific situation of the psalm—nevertheless it should be observed that some of the motifs found in these accounts also appear in Ps. 31:10–14, and form parts of descriptions of misery in Job and Lamentations.

Psalm 6:6 displays a "death"-motif, v. 11 refers to "enemies"—as "the power of death" and "enemies" are listed as common elements in the "royal passion"—or "Ebed YHWH"-psalms (cf. A 2.1, 4) the distribution and import of these motifs must be scrutinized:

1.1.1. In the starting group the "death"-motif appears in metaphors (Ps. 28:1, 31:13, 88:5, 143:7), in questions addressed to YHWH (Ps. 6:6, 30:10, 88:11 ff.), in references to the activities of a third party (Ps. 143:3), in accounts of salvation (Ps. 56:14, 86:13, 116:8—cf. also 30:4), and in descriptions of distress, often combined with references to "water" (Jon. 2:4, 6–7b, Ps. 18:5–6, 116:3a–b—cf. also Ps. 69:2–3, 15–16). Some of these categories overlap—metaphors for instance may be incorporated in descriptions of misery (cf. Ps. 88:5 within the section 88:2/3–10a).

The metaphors are divided into two groups: in Ps. 28:1d and 143:7d (in formulaic language) they depict the negative consequences that would follow if YHWH would fail to comply with the preceding exhortations—i.e. forsakenness and dying/death are seen as equivalents in context—while in Ps. 31:13a and 88:5a they represent one component in detailed descriptions of misery. Ps. 31:10–14 speaks of sorrow, absence of friends and "plotting"; Ps. 88:4–5, forming motivations for the exhortations of v. 3, refers to the psalmist as being "on the brink of Sheol" and compares him to "those who go down to the Pit", vv. 6–7, developing the metaphor, place him among "the dead", "the slaughtered in their graves", "those forgotten/deprived"—this condition being caused by YHWH's "anger" and his "waves" (cf. Jon. 2:4), v. 9 refers to the absence of friends. Similar motifs are found in the section 14–19: vv. 17–18 speak of "anger", which is compared with "waters", v. 19 mentions abandonment. Common to Ps. 31:10–14 and 88:2/3–10 is that they contain relevant formulaic language only at the outset of the sections (Ps. 31:10a(–b), 10c, 11a, 88:3a, b).

In the units mainly conforming to compositional convention (Pss. 28, 143) "forsakenness"/"death" caused by potential isolation from YHWH is only one of several thematically unrelated motivations for different exhortations, whereas the "death"-motifs of Ps. 31:13 and 88:5, forming part of non-formulaic descriptions of misery, are integrated with the context: Ps. 31:10–14 and 88:2/3–10, 14–19 combine "death" and "forsakenness" but refer to isolation from friends and acquaintances, the utmost reason for which being human "plotting" (Ps. 31:14) or divine wrath (Ps. 88:8, 17—cf. also Jb. 19).

The questions addressed to YHWH are preceded by descriptions of the invocational situation in Pss. 30 and 88; the stanzas 30:10 and 88:11 ff. contain four components each, while the simple question of Ps. 6:6b may be seen as a prolongation of the motivation for preceding imperatives.

Ps. 6 and 30:9–13 display only these realizations of the "death"-motif, and the conclusions of the units lack references to "saving"; Ps. 6:9, 10 speak of YHWH's having "heard" the prayers of the psalmist, Ps. 30:12 tells of sorrow turned into gladness—this indicates that Ps. 6:6b and 30:10 should be considered stylistical means of inducement (cf. also Is. 38:18).

In Ps. 30 the "death"-motif recurs within the section 2–4/5–6, which presents traits indicating an exilic/post-exilic time of origin (cf. K 4.1.2.1). Here the questions of v. 10 are turned into statements concerning accomplished salvation, i.e. re-establishment and life.

Ps. 88 contains three references to the invocational situation (v. 2, 10 b–c, 14), and it is difficult to decide whether these initiate originally independent sections, or whether they should be considered conscious repetitions. vv. 11–13 however, are well integrated in the main theme of the psalm; since vv. 3–10a and 15–19 outline the personal misery of the psalmist, comparing his situation to a state of dying/death (cf. above), vv. 11–13 may be seen as a reflexion of the same situation, although the section lacks first person sing references.

Within the starting group, the only reference to a "death"-motif connected with activities of a hostile third party is found in Ps. 143:3 (cf. also Ps. 7:6). Culley records this stanza and Lm. 3:6 as "possibly related" (1967:89, no. 170) on the grounds of similar terminology. There is however a notable difference between the two—the cause of the misery reported in Ps. 143 being an "enemy", and in Lm. 3 YHWH (cf. also Ps. 88:2/3–10a). Whatever the import of "darkness", Ps. 143:3 is a metaphor, comparing the situation of the psalmist with that of "the dead long ago".

In accounts of salvation the "death"-motif is found in Ps. 56:14, 86:13 and 116:8 (cf. also 30:4) within the starting group. Of these Ps. 56:14 and 116:8–9 show far-reaching terminological similarities; furthermore, in Ps. 56 YHWH is enjoined to "take pity"—one of the motivations referring to a third party "determined to take my life" (v. 7), in Ps. 116 YHWH is asked to "rescue" against a background of "death's cords", "the sorrows/nooses of Sheol" (vv. 3 a–b, cf. below). Thus, in Pss. 56 and 116 a correspondence between exhortations, descriptions of distress, and accounts of salvation can be discerned, while Ps. 86: 1–13, presenting a variety of exhortations and motivations, only displays a "death"-motif in the final motivation. It was mentioned above (K 5) that Ps. 86 is the only example within the starting group of a formulaic psalm deviating from the basic pattern; it was pointed out that the contents of vv. 8 and 9–10 indicate an exilic/post-exilic date for the unit in its present form. The lack of correspondence between exhortations–motivations and the account of salvation suggest that Ps. 86 is a compilation of traditional invocational language, where only the non-formulaic parts indicate the time and situation of the present psalm.

In accounts of distress the "death"-motif is often combined with references to "water" (Ps. 18: 5–6, 116: 3 a–b, Jon. 2: 4 b–c, 6–7 b—cf. also Ps. 69: 2–3, 15–16). In Pss. 18 and 116 the distress is depicted as waves/torrents/cords of death/Belial/Sheol, whereas Jon. 2 speaks of flood/waves/billows etc. and refers to the sphere of "death" only in the accounts of accomplished salvation (v. 3, 8).

Psalms 18: 5–6 and 116: 3 a–b are preceded by introductions and followed by references to the invocational situation, leading up to exhortations. Ps. 18: 17–20 enjoins YHWH to "take", "draw", the psalmist "from the deep waters", to "deliver" him from a powerful "enemy" and to "free" and "rescue" him against the background of "love" (v. 20 b; ki and perf 3sg); Ps. 116 contains only one exhortation, which lacks motivation ("rescue" in v. 4, followed by a section showing hymnic traits—cf. K 3.2.1.3).

In Ps. 116: 1–9 the correspondence is total between account of distress, exhortation, and conclusion (cf. above), while Ps. 18: 2–7, 17–20 together with "water/death" mentions "enemies" (v. 18 f.) as a cause of distress, contains exhortations pertaining to both these obstacles, and lacks references to accomplished salvation. The lack of a "conclusion" however may be explained against the background outlined above (K 4.1.1)—i.e. in a combination of units of different origin the conclusion of the basic "lament" may have been omitted in favor of vv. 47–49/50.

In Ps. 69 motifs from the section 2–6 recur in vv. 14–16 (and 17–20; cf. K 3.1.3.2 and n. F 7), and the terminology of the sections coincides to such a degree as to make a conscious repetition plausible (cf. מעמקי מים in v. 3 and 5, שבלת in v. 3 and 16, שנאי in v. 5 and 15—cf. also איבי in v. 5 and 19); vv. 14–17 refer to water in connexion with "the grave"[3] and mentions "those who hate me"—YHWH is summoned to "answer", "pull out", "let escape", "save", and not to let "the waves wash over me", "the deep swallow me" or "the Pit close its mouth on me"; vv. 2–6, initiated by an exhortation to "save", speak of "waters", "swamp", "waves", "exhaustion", and "those who hate me". The unit lacks references to accomplished salvation.

Jon. 2 seems to be a chiastic composition (cf. above n. F 15), where the accounts of (invocation and) salvation (v. 3, 8) speak of YHWH's having "heard" the prayers of the supplicant, uttered in a situation referred to as "the belly of Sheol" or "my soul (was) fainting in me"—this miserable condition (vv. 4b–c, 6–7b: "flood", "waves", etc.) being brought about by YHWH (v. 4a: "you cast me in the abyss"), but also remedied by him (v. 7c: "you lifted my life from the Pit").

The real problem, as expressed in the focal stanza (v. 5), is however "isolation", and the references to "water/death" may thus be seen as metaphors, depicting a condition allegedly caused by YHWH. Such metaphors are also found in Ps. 88 (cf. above); furthermore Ps. 88: 2/3–10a and 14–19 show terminological similarities to Jon. 2 (cf. מצלות in Ps. 88: 7—מצולה in Jon. 2: 4, סבב in 88: 18, Jon. 2: 4, 6, משבריך in 88: 8, Jon. 2: 4, עלי עברו in 88: 17, Jon. 2: 4), and contain an "isolation"-motif—this however referring to the absence of friends and acquaintances (Ps. 88: 9, 19).

The units referring to "water/death" in accounts of distress can be subdivided into two categories; one mentioning the obstacles and asking for remedy (Ps. 18, 69, 116), the other tracing the origins of a troublesome situation back to YHWH, and lacking exhortations (Jon. 2, Ps. 88).

1.1.1.2. The majority of the realizations of the ("water"/)"death"-motif are seen as metaphors, accounting for hypothetical isolation from YHWH (Ps. 28: 1d, 143: 7d) or actual isolation from fellow human beings (Ps. 31: 13a), a troublesome situation caused by a hostile third party (Ps. 143: 3) or by YHWH (Jon. 2: 4b–c, 6–7b, Ps. 88: 5f., 7f., 18—cf. also 88: 11–13), or as stylistic means of inducement—metaphors or stylistic devices are, however, of little relevance in the search for themes/motifs reflecting the components of a ritual.

The metaphors proper have no equivalents in the Servant Songs of Deutero-Isaiah, but the "forsakenness" referred to in the immediate non-formulaic contexts of Ps. 31: 13 and 88: 5 may be compared to Is. 53: 3: "A thing despised and rejected by men, a man of sorrows and familiar with suffering, a man to make people screen their faces; he was despised and we took no account of him" (cf. also Ps. 69: 9, 21). Psalms 18, 69 and 116 refer to "water/death" in accounts of distress; Ps. 116 mentions only this obstacle (vv. 3a–b), and describes the situation as one of "anguish and distress" (v. 3c: צרה ויגון), Pss. 18 and 69 combine the motif with that of a "hostile third party" (cf. especially Ps. 69: 15), describing the situation as one of "distress" (Ps. 18:7, 69:18: צר). In Ps. 116 the psalmist asks to be "rescued" (v. 4) and the account of salvation refers to YHWH's having "treated kindly/rescued" (v. 8b, 9a), Pss. 18 and 69 contain exhortations pertaining both to "water/death" and to a "hostile third party", but lack explicit accounts of salvation.

Ps. 18:5–6, 69:2–3, 15–16 and 116:3a–b are the only realizations within the Book of Psalms of a "water/death"-motif where the distress described is not envisaged as inflicted by YHWH. The realities behind these descriptions are difficult to specify, but the qualifications "anguish"/"distress" and the references to "enemies" and "haters" in context indicate a metaphorical use of the motif.

Psalms 18:(2–4), 5–7, 17–20 and 116:(1–2), 3–9 conform to the compositional convention/tradition and may be ascribed similar settings; Ps. 69:2–6, 14–16/17–20, 30–31 are related to the two through the use of similar motifs, while the small proportion of relevant formulaic language indicates a specific situation, or a time and situation when the compositional convention was not relevant (cf. K 4.2.2). Psalms 18 and 116 were offered as examples of psalms constituting or reflecting a ritual—a ritual or liturgical collection which provided the "Vorlage" of the Ebed YHWH-songs of Deutero-Isaiah (cf. A 2.2, 2.1). Yet these Songs present neither motifs nor terminology akin to that of Ps. 18:(2–4), 5–7, 17–20 and 116:(1–2), 3–9, and thus no relationship can be proved.

1.1.2.1. Within the starting group the "enemy"-motif is realized in brief references to "oppressors", "haters", "evil-doers", etc., in introductions or summaries (Ps. 25:2, 30:2, 31:16), in sections characterized by exhortations with motivations (Ps. 18:18, 25:19, 61:4, 69:19, 71:4, 10, 142:7, 143:3, 9, 12), in detailed descriptions of misery (Ps. 22:17, 31:12, 69:5, 102:8), in concluding motivations (Ps. 31:9), and in wishes (Ps. 6:11, 31:18f., 71:13, 86:17); references to "wicked" are found in accounts of innocence (Ps. 26:9–10, 28:3–5), while the more substantial wishes concerning a third party (Ps. 69:23–29, 109:6–20—cf. also 17:13–14, 140:10–12) tend to lack specifications. Detailed accounts of the activities of a hostile third party are found in Ps. 17:8/9–12, 56:2–3, 6(–10), 109:1–5, and 140: 2–6.

In introductions or summaries, sections containing exhortations with motivations, and in concluding motivations איב is used to designate the third party (with the exception of Ps. 71:4, 142:7, 143:12), while detailed descriptions of misery, accounts of the activities of a hostile third party, and sections containing wishes show a varied terminology.

The "enemies", "oppressors", etc., are reported as engaging in oral, mental, or (attempts at) physical attacks; they gloat, conspire, utter threats, hate, assail or show hostility (for Ps. 143:3 cf. above)—the references are however too short and show contents too general to convey information as to the actual scope of the activities.

Within the mainly non-formulaic sections containing detailed accounts of personal misery (Ps. 22:12–17/18–19, 31:10–14, 69:8/9–13, 21–22, 102:5–12, 109:21–25—cf. also 22:7–11) one of the obstacles mentioned is a hostile third party defined as "a gang of villains" (Ps. 22:17), "oppressors" (Ps. 31:12), "enemies" (Ps. 102:8) or only referred to in the third person plural—they "glare at me, gloating / they divide my garments among them and cast lots for my clothes" (Ps. 22:18b–19), ("I hear their endless slanders, threats from every quarter, as) they combine against me, plotting to take my life" (Ps. 31:14), "... gave me poison to eat instead, when I was thirsty they gave me vinegar to drink" (Ps. 69:22), or "I become their laughing-stock, the gossip of people sitting at the city gate, and the theme of drunken songs" (Ps. 69:13), "I have become an object of derision, people shake their heads at me in scorn" (Ps. 109:25). All the references to an undefined third party conclude their units. The introduction of Ps. 22 (vv. 2–11, cf. above n. F 56) contains a short description of personal misery (vv. 7–9), showing motifs similar to those of Ps. 109:25: ("Yet here I am, now more worm than man, scorn of mankind, jest of the people) / all who see me jeer at me, they toss their heads and sneer" (vv. 7–8).

A majority of the short realizations of the "enemy"-motif are found in units conforming to the compositional convention/tradition (Ps. 6:11, 18:18, 71:4, 10, 143:3, 9, 12—for 22:17, 31:12 and 102:9 cf. above), others appear in units adhering to the basic pattern but indicating special situations (Ps. 61:4), in such suggesting a time and situation when the compositional convention was not yet developed or no longer relevant (Ps. 25:19, 86:17), or in units differing structurally and linguistically from the main group (Ps. 25:2, 26:9f., 142:7). As short references to a hostile third party are very common also outside the starting group (cf. Ps. 3:8, 8:3, 9:4, 7, 13:3, 5, 43:2, 44:17, 45:6, 54:9, 55:4, 68:24, 89:23, 106:10, 127:5 etc.), this phenomenon cannot be said to constitute an element characteristic of a specific setting.

The more substantial references to a third party or descriptions of hostile activity directed against the psalmist are found in sections lacking relevant formulaic language (Ps. 69:23–29, 109:6–20, 17:13–14, 140:10–12; 17:8/9–12, 56:2–3, 6ff., 109:1–5, 140:2–6). The "Fluch"-sections of Pss. 69 and 109 do not give names to the third party, the descriptions of Pss. 17, 56, 109 and 140 use varying designations—it should however be noted that איב appears only once (Ps. 17:9) as against fifteen times in the "short

102

references", while רשע is found three times (Ps. 17: 13, 109: 2, 140: 5).[4] The activities of the adversaries are described as oral or physical—in Ps. 17: 8/9–12, 56: 6ff., 109: 1–5 and 140: 2–6 references to both are found, while Ps. 56: 2–3 and 140: 10–12 only mention violence or attempts at violence; the only hostile operation reported in the "Fluch"-sections tells of a third party "hounding a man after you have struck him, adding more wounds to those which you afflicted" (Ps. 69: 27). No uniform terminology can be discerned within the group.

The sections containing wishes concerning a third party, or descriptions of hostile activity directed against the psalmist, do not conform to the compositional convention/tradition; Pss. 56 and 140 lack both structural and formulaic similarities to the main group, Pss. 17: 6c–15 and 109 indicate a time and situation without a vivid compositional convention, Ps. 69 presents a kernel of formulaic language. Wishes and descriptions of hostile activity are also found in units not included in the starting group (cf. Ps. 10: 2–11, 35: 4–8, 11–16, 19–21, 36: 4–5, 58: 4–7/8–9, 59: 2–6/7–10, 12–16, 64: 2–7, 73: 2–12, Jr. 18: 19–23, Jb. 18: 5–21, 20: 4–29, etc.)—a fact which confirms the implication that the "enemy"-motif is a constituent with various realizations to be found in various contexts.

Within the starting group references to animals are found in the non-formulaic account of distress of Ps. 22: 12–17/18–19 (vv. 13–14, 17—cf. also vv. 21–22). The psalmist is surrounded by different kinds of "bulls" (v. 13, 22), "lions" (v. 17,[5] 21), and "dogs" (v. 17, 21)—the כלבים of v. 17 a seem however to be parallel to the עדת מרעים of v. 17 b. As Ps. 22 contains the only realizations of this motif within the starting group—Ps. 17: 12 and 140: 4 *compare* the activities of a third party with that of animals (cf. also Ps. 7: 3, 35: 17, 57: 5)—no comments will be made on the import of the different categories mentioned.

1.1.2.2. The short realizations of the "enemy"-motif are found in units included in the starting group, but also in a great number of psalms outside this group. Common to both categories is that the references are too brief and show contents too general to convey information as to the actual scope of the activities reported; furthermore, the various functions and the wide distribution make it difficult to characterize the motif as special for any defined group of psalms.

Within the starting group the wishes concerning a third party are preceded by detailed descriptions of hostile activity in Pss. 17, 109 and 140. In Pss. 17 and 140 a correspondence of designations of the third party in the descriptions and in the wishes can be isolated, while the "Fluch"-sections of Pss. 69 and 109 lack terminological and thematical connexions to preceding contexts. Substantial references to a third party are also found outside the starting group, but the activities reported vary to such a degree that a common ritual origin is hardly plausible.

The Servant Songs of Deutero-Isaiah contain only indirect references to hostile activity: "I offered my back to those who struck me, my cheeks to those who tore at my beard; I did not cover my face against insult and spittle" (Is. 50:6), "... despised and rejected by men ..." (Is. 53:3)—these references may be compared to Ps. 22:7b–8: "... scorn of mankind, jest of the people / all who see me jeer at me, they toss their heads and sneer" (cf. also Ps. 109:25). Ps. 22:2–11 and 109:21–25 are mainly non-formulaic and seen as "deviations" from the basic pattern—thus they cannot be offered as examples of a compositional convention; the units which do adhere to such a convention show neither terminological nor thematical similarities to the Servant Songs, which makes the theory of "Vorlage" and "Nachdichtung" (cf. above 1.1.1.2) unrealistic.

1.2.1. Ps. 18:(2–4), 5–7, 17–20 mentions "the waves of death", "the torrents of Belial", "the cords of Sheol", "the snares of death", "a powerful enemy", and "a foe too strong for me", and refers to the situation as one of "distress". Even though "the day of my disaster" (v. 19a) is an unusual designation (cf. Dt. 32:35, Ob. 13×3; Jb. 21:30) the references to a third party are too brief and show contents too general to indicate the actual scope of the hostile activities; the realities behind "the waves/torrents" etc., are difficult to specify, but the epitome "distress" points towards a metaphorical use of the motif (cf. above 1.1.1.1).

Thus, from the descriptions of distress and the references to a third party no conclusions can be drawn as to the specific setting of Ps. 18:(2–4), 5–7, 17–20, nor can a relationship to the Servant Songs of Deutero-Isaiah be established (cf. above 1.1.1.2).

1.2.2. For Ps. 18:8–16 cf. n. F 59 and K 6, for vv. 21–25, 26–30/31, 31/32–46, 47–50 and 51 cf. K 3.1.3.2 and 4.1.1. These sections lack themes/motifs akin to those found in the Servant Songs (for Ps. 18:32a cf. however Is. 44:7, 45:21).

1.3.1. Ps. 28:3 refers to the deceit of "wicked" and "evil men" in a general wording, v. 4 asks for retribution using equally general expressions, while v. 5 specifies the deficiencies of the third party; they are "blind to the works of Yahweh, to his own handwork"—therefore, "may he pull them down and not rebuild them!". An equivalent to v. 5a is found in Is. 5:12b: "... never a thought for the works of Yahweh, never a glance for what his hands have done"—therefore, "my people will go into exile" (Is. 5:13a);

vv. 5b–c show a terminology similar to that of Jr. 18:7, 9, 31:28, 42:10 (cf. also Jr. 1:10, 45:4)—all found in sections dealing with future or present expatriation (cf. Jr. 18:11, 17, 24:5, 31:23, 27). From these implications of v. 5 it may be suggested that the "wicked" and "evil men" were seen as preparing the way for national catastrophe through their lack of insight and perception; such a setting would indicate a pre-exilic origin of the unit. Ps. 28:(1–2), 3–7, show no thematical similarities to the Servant Songs.

1.3.2. For Ps. 28:8 cf. K 3.1.6.1, for v. 9 K 3.1.6.5. These addenda show neither themes nor motifs akin to those of the Servant Songs.

1.4.1. In Ps. 31:2c–9 the exhortations and the account of salvation give no detailed information about the situation of the psalmist; the motivations containing expressions of confidence and the indirect references to hostile activity are too brief and show contents too general to permit conclusions as to the setting of the unit.

Ps. 31:2c–9 (with vv. 15–18b—cf. K 4.1.1) shows neither themes nor motifs akin to those of the Servant Songs.

1.4.2. Between Ps. 31:2c–9 and 15–18b is found a section containing formulaic language only at the outset, and showing themes/motifs differing from those of vv. 2c–9 (15–18b). This section is initiated by exhortations motivated by short references to general distress (cf. Ps. 6:3, 69:18, 102:3, Lm. 1:20, etc.), followed by a detailed account of personal misery. The afflictions are described as sorrow and "physical inconvenience"[6] (cf. Ps. 102:4, and *comm. ad* Ps. 6:3 above), contempt and forsakenness (cf. Ps. 22:7, 8, 38:12, 44:14, 15, 69:9, 71:7, 79:4, 88:9, 19, 109:25, Is. 53:3, Jb. 19:13ff.), horror, and plotting (cf. Jr. 20:10; cf. also Jr. 6:25, 20:3f., 46:5, 49:29, Lm. 2:22, 3:61f.). As to structure and contents vv. 10–14 may be compared with the units 69:7/8–13, 21–22 and 109:21–25 (cf. also Ps. 22:7ff., 12–17/18–19); furthermore, some of the motifs of the mainly non-formulaic unit also appear in Jr., Jb. and Lm. (for "forsakenness" cf. above 1.1.2.1).

1.4.3. For Ps. 31:18c–19, 20–21, 22–23, 24/25 cf. above 4.1.1. With the exception of the possibly related נגרזתי (Ps. 31:23)—נגזר (Is. 53:8; cf. also נגזרתי in Lm. 3:54, נגזרו in Ps. 88:6, and נגרשתי in Jon. 2:5) these sections contain neither thematical nor terminological similarities to the Servant Songs.

1.5.1. Ps. 71:2–5 contains positive exhortations with references to a third party, motivated by utterances of confidence, vv. 9–11 present negative exhortations with references to "old age", motivated by accounts of hostile activity, vv. 12–13 contain both negative and positive exhortations, followed by modal impfa expressing wishes concerning a third party, v. 22 displays modal impfa 1sg.

The positive exhortations and the utterances of confidence show a stereotyped terminology, the only exceptions being מעוֹל and חוֹמץ (v. 4), appearing as parallels to רשע, and the reference to "trust from youth" (v. 5); the mainly non-formulaic negative exhortations with references to "old age" (v. 9) and motivations specify the situation (note the quotation in v. 11): an old man, always having trusted YHWH, finds himself surrounded by adversaries, who, claiming that YHWH has deserted him, try to take advantage of the situation—now the old man needs support, and he expresses himself in traditional language (vv. 2–5, 12–13, 22).

Ps. 71:2–5, 9–11, 12–13, 22, (Ps. 71 A) shows neither terminological nor thematical similarities to the Servant Songs of Deutero-Isaiah.

1.5.2. Ps. 71:6–7, 14–15/16–19a, 23–24a (Ps. 71 B) may be read as a coherent unit with uniform terminology (cf. K 1.3.1.3); this unit, lacking relevant formulaic language, seems to have been combined with the "lament" proper for thematical reasons—both cover a period "from youth to old age", (cf. K 4.1.1) but, while Ps. 71 A is entreating, Ps. 71 B portrays a man, who, having relied on YHWH since the time of his birth, or even before that (cf. Is. 49:1, Ps. 22:10f.—cf. also Is. 44:2, 24, 46:3), will always praise him. Even though "many" have seen him as an "enigma"[7] (cf. Is. 49:7, 52:14, 53:3, Ps. 31:12), YHWH is his refuge. His only prayer, now that he is "old and grey" (cf. Is. 46:4), is to be given enough time to proclaim YHWH's "arm", "strength", and "righteousness" to (coming) generations (cf. Ps. 22:31, 32, 102:19). For Ps. 71:2–5, 9–11, 12–13 and 22 cf. above 1.5.1. Thus several of the motifs of the non-formulaic Ps. 71 B are also found in Deutero-Isaiah (cf. especially Is. 46:3–4), some even within the Servant Songs (cf. Ps. 71:6–Is. 49:1, 71:7–Is. 49:7, 52:14); others appear in psalms which, according to Becker (cf. K 3.1.6.2), have been subjected to exilic/post-exilic "Neuinterpretation" (cf. Ps. 71:6–22:10f., 71:18–22:31, 32, 102:19).

For vv. 19b–20/21 cf. K 4.1.1.

1.6. In Ps. 116:(1–2), 3–9 accounts of distress and invocational situation precede the exhortation (cf. K 3.1.1)—v. 3 mentions "death's cords" and "the sorrows/nooses of Sheol", referring to the situation as one of "anguish and distress"—this indicates a metaphorical use of the "water/death"-motif (cf. above 1.1.1.1). No conclusions can be drawn as to the specific setting of the unit, nor can a relationship to the Servant Songs of Deutero-Isaiah be established (cf. above 1.1.1.2). vv. 10–19 are related to the "lament" proper through a common terminology; the section recapitulates a (former)[8] situation of distress, accounts for the relief, and states the personal consequences thereof (cf. above n. F 9): "I was completely crushed", "I declared in my alarm: no man can be relied on", but YHWH "showed goodness" and "loosened my fetters"—therefore "I will lift the cup of salvation", and "offer you the thanksgiving sacrifice" "in the presence of all his people", "in the courts of the house of Yahweh".

vv. 10c–11 correspond to vv. 3a–b, v. 12b and 16c to vv. 7b–8, and v. 13f. and 17f. to v. 9; i.e. being surrounded by "death's cords", etc. is seen as the equivalent of being "crushed" and "alarmed", being "rescued" is compared to having "the fetters loosened", and "walking in Yahweh's presence in the land of the living" is connected with "offering of the thanksgiving sacrifice" (cf. Ps. 56: 13f.)—as there also seems to be a certain correspondence between the subsections 10–14 and 16–18 the "lifting of the cup of salvation" and the "offering" may indicate cognate procedures.

The terminology of vv. 10–14, 15, 16–18, and 19 is uncommon: ענה[II] (Qal, perf 1sg) appears only in Ps. 116: 10, תגמול only in 116: 12, כוס ישועות only in 116: 13 and מוסר (I) in 116: 16, Is. 28: 22, 52:2 and Jb.12:18—thus the exact purport of the situation and proceedings reported remains unclear.

Ps. 116: 16 describes the psalmist as "your servant, your servant, the son of your maid-servant", Is. 42: 1, 5, 6 and 53: 10 refer to "my servant". While the former is a designation, inferring dependence and subjection (cf. also Ex. 23: 12, Gn. 14: 14, 17: 12), the latter is an assignation, implying a wide-ranging mission.

Ps. 116 shows neither themes nor motifs akin to those of the Servant Songs.


1.7. In Ps. 143 the references to personal distress are too brief and show contents too general to permit any conclusions as to the actual scope of the afflictions (for v. 3 and 7d cf. above 1.1.1.1), and the expressions of confidence show a stereotyped language; v. 2b, 8c and 10a show motifs otherwise not common in "individual laments" (for v. 2b cf. Jb. 4: 17, 9: 12, 15: 14; for v. 8a and 10c cf. Ps. 25: 4, 5, 119: 12, 26, 64, 66, 68, 108, 124, 135—cf. also Ex. 33: 13) but give no exact information concerning the setting of the unit.

In v. 12c the designation "your servant" is used to prevail upon YHWH to intervene on behalf of the speaker. The servant requests "the help that his master ought to give him in virtue of the relationship between them"[9] (cf. also v. 10b); the psalmist's state of dependence within this relationship is underlined through the prayer not to be judged with the strictness of the law (v. 2 a)—in his own strength he cannot fulfil the demands of YHWH. For the use of "my servant" in the Servant Songs cf. above 1.6.

Ps. 143 contains neither themes nor motifs akin to those of the Servant Songs.

2.1.1. In virtue of a common structure Ps. 6, 18: (2–4), 5–7, 17–20, 28: (1–2), 3–7, 31: (2 a–b), 2 c–9, (15–18 b), 71: (1), 2–5, 9–13, 22, 116: (1–2), 3–9 (10–19), and 143 may be seen as realizations of a basic "Schema", but as the exhortations to "save", "listen", "lead and keep", etc., motivated by expressions of confidence, references to the character or attributes of YHWH, and short statements concerning the situation, character or actions of the psalmist contain motifs not restricted to units conforming to the compositional convention/tradition, no common, specific setting can be ascertained for this "Schema"; the isolation of formal, linguistic elements (cf. G 1.1) has thus led to the identification of motifs common to invocational tradition.

The set language and general contents of Ps. 6, 18: (2–4), 5–7, 17–20, 31: (2 a–b), 2 c–9, (15–18 b), 116: (1–2), 3–9, and 143 indicate a function as formulas with general applicability in situations of distress—Pss. 28 and 71 A outline such situations using non-formulaic language, but apply set phrases in the prayers for remedy (for Ps. 116: 10–19 cf. above 1.6)—thus the designation "rituals", directly referring to the cultic function of the sacral king and "pertaining to the Annual Festival" cannot be sustained. The lack of criteria for identifying the subject and specifying the setting of these units also makes the designation "Ebed YHWH-psalms" inappropriate (cf. A 3); furthermore, since the Ebed YHWH-songs of Deutero-Isaiah were characterized as a "prophetic 'Nachdichtung' from a liturgical collection pertaining to the Annual Festival" (A 2.2), it is not surprising to find that, due to the lack of common themes/motifs, no relationship can be established between units conforming to the compositional convention/ tradition and the Servant Songs.


2.1.2. Ps. 31: 10–14 outlines a situation of distress and misery; the afflictions are described as sorrow, physical inconvenience, contempt, forsakenness, horror, and plotting. This mainly non-formulaic section shows a "Horizont" similar to that of Ps. 69: 7/8–13, 21–22 and 109: 21–25 (cf. also Ps. 22: 7 ff., 12–17/18–19), and contains motifs also found in "national laments", Is. 53, Jr., Jb. and Lm., but differs, as to structure and contents, from vv. (2 a–b), 2 c–9, (15–18 b). At this stage of the investigation no criteria are available for identifying the subject or specifying the setting of the unit.

Ps. 71: 6–7, 14–15/16–19 a, 23–24 a, (Ps. 71 B) may be read as a separate unit with uniform terminology.

Several of the motifs of this non-formulaic unit are also found in Deutero-Isaiah, some even within the Servant Songs; others appear in psalms which, according to Becker (1966), have been subjected to exilic/post-exilic "Neuinterpretation". At this stage of the investigation no criteria are available for identifying the subject or specifying the setting of the unit.

Ps. 28: 8 and 18: 51 both display a "king/Messiah"-motif, but, whereas Ps. 18 in its present form may be interpreted as a "royal thanksgiving" in the light of v. 51 (and vv. 31/32–50), Ps. 28: 8 does not give rise to such a designation (cf. K 3.1.6.1). Even though the liturgical subject of Ps. 18 may be identified as the king, and motifs otherwise associated with the Annual Festival may be isolated, the psalm displays no "ideological" (cf. A 2.1) similarities to the Servant Songs, and thus the theory of "Vorlage"–"Nachdichtung" (A 2.2) must be rejected.

3. Summing up: units conforming to the compositional convention / tradition may be seen as realizations of a basic "Schema"; the set language and general contents of these units indicate a function as formulas with general applicability in situations of distress. The lack of criteria for identification of subject and specification of setting within the group disproves both the designation "Ebed YHWH-psalms" and the qualifications "rituals, directly referring to the cultic function of the sacral king", and "pertaining to the Annual Festival". No relationship can be established between Ps. 6, 18: (2–4), 5–7, 17–20, 31: (2 a–b), 2 c–9, (15–18 b), 71: (1), 2–5, 9–13, 22, 116: (1–2), 3–9, (10–19), 143 and the Servant Songs of Deutero-Isaiah.

In its present form Ps. 18 may be identified as a "royal thanksgiving", but, even though motifs otherwise associated with the Annual Festival may be isolated, the designation "Ebed YHWH" is misleading; the psalm lacks "ideological" similarities to the Servant Songs—thus the theory of "Vorlage"–"Nachdichtung" must be rejected.

Two mainly non-formulaic units, i.e. Ps. 31: 10–14, and 71: 6–7, 14–15/ 16–19 a, 23–24 a, found within psalms conforming to the compositional convention/tradition, but differing from the "laments" proper in structure and contents do however display subject matter akin to that found in the Servant Songs, in Jr., Lm., and Jb., in "national laments", and in psalms suspected of having been subjected to exilic/post-exilic "Neuinterpretation". Further investigation of these units must precede a specification of setting and of the relationship to the texts of Deutero-Isaiah. My interest will be directed towards Ps. 31: 10–14.

# M. TRADITION AND INTERPRETATION

1. Two different modes of invocation were isolated above: one, where formulaic exhortations to "save", etc. and short motivations containing expressions of confidence, references to the character or attributes of YHWH, and statements concerning the situation, character or actions of the psalmist are evenly distributed (K 1.1); another, where injunctions to "listen" or "answer", etc. lead into detailed, mainly non-formulaic descriptions of personal misery (K 1.2). In the second group expressions of confidence and references to YHWH's attributes or character are lacking.

Set phrases express general ideas, and thus a specification of setting for the first group (K 1.1) is impossible; non-formulaic language is used to outline specific situations—to determine whether the second group (K 1.2) reflects a separate literary convention, a scrutiny of the elements of subject matter within the non-formulaic sections is necessary.

In the following an inventory will be made of the constitutive elements of Ps. 31: 10–14 and similarities of motif to other units noted. If, along with certain structural similarities, motifs common to a number of units can be isolated,[1] it seems reasonable to suppose that these units reflect a common cultural background, and a literary convention within that background.

1.1.1. Ps. 31

10 a–b "Take pity (because) I am in trouble": Ps. *6:3,*[2] *25:16, 69:18, 102:3, Lm. 1:20;* cf. also Ps. 18: 7, 106: 44, 107: 6, 13, 19, 28 in accounts of salvation.

10 c–11 "grief wastes away my eye, my throat, my inmost parts / for my life is worn out with sorrow, my years with sighs; my strength yields under misery, my bones are wasting away": Ps. 6:*7, 8,* 22: 15–16 b, 18 a, 38: 7–11, 102:*4–*6, 109: 22 b–23, Jr. 9: 18, (14: 7), 45: 3, Jb. 3: 24, 19: 20, 30: 17, 30, Lm. (1: 11, 2: 11), 5: 17.

12–13 "To every one of my oppressors I am contemptible, (loathsome) to my neighbours. Those who see me in the street hurry past me; / I am forgotten, as good as dead in their hearts, something discarded": Ps. 22: 7–8(9), 38: 12, 44: 14, 69: 9, 79: 4, 88: (5), 9, 19, 89: 42, 51, 109: 25, Is. 52: 14, 53: 3, Jr. 9: 19, 15: 15, 17, 20: 7 f., (24: 9), (Dn. 9: 16), Jb. 16: 20, 17: 2, 6 (19: 13 ff.), Lm. 3: 61, (5: 1).

14 "I hear their endless slanders, threats from every quarter, as they combine against me, plotting to take my life": Ps. 38: 13, 41: 6 ff., 71: 10 f.;
Jr. 11: 19, 20: 10 (cf. also Jr. 6: 25, 20: 3 f., 46: 5, 49: 29, Lm. 2: 22), Jb. 16:
9 f., Lm. 3: 60–62.

1.1.2. Elements of subject matter, found in Ps. 31: 10–14, recur in the sections 22: 7–11, 12–17/18–19, 38: 7–13, 88: 2–3/4–10 a, 14/15–19, 102: 2–4/
5–12, 109: 21–25, and, scattered, in Pss. 6, 25, 41, 44, 69, 71, 79, 89,
in Is. 52, 53, Jr. 9, 11, 15, 24, in Jb. 3, 16, 17, 19, 30, and in Lm. 1, 3,
and 5.

To determine whether the substantial, mainly non-formulaic sections
of Pss. 22, 38, 88, 102, and 109 might be ascribed a common "Horizont",
the subject matter of these units must be investigated, and similarities
of theme/motifs to other units noted; Ps. 69: 8/9–13 and 21–22 will also
be included in the group (cf. K 3.1.4.1, 4.1.1).

1.1.2.1. Ps. 22
7–8(9) "Yet here I am, more worm than man, scorn of mankind, jest of
the people / all who see me jeer at me, they toss their heads and sneer
(/ 'He relied on Yahweh, let Yahweh save him! If Yahweh is his friend,
let Him rescue him')": Ps. 31: 12, 44: 14 f., 79: 4, 89: 42, 51, Is. (37: 22,
49: 7, 52: 14), 53: 3, Jr. (9: 19; 15: 15), 18: 16, (20: 7 f.; 24: 9), (Ob. 12),
Jb. (16: 20), 17: 2, 6, Lm. 2: 15. For תולעת cf. Is. 41: 14.
10–11 "Yet you drew me out of the womb, you entrusted me to my mother's
breasts / placed on your lap from my birth, from my mother's womb you
have been my God": Ps. 71: 6 (cf. also Is. 44: 2, 24, 46: 3, 49: 1, 5; Jr. 1: 5).

1.1.2.2. Ps. 22
12 "Do not stand aside: trouble is near, I have no one to help me": Ps.
*35: 22, 38: 22, 71: 12;* 69: 21, Lm. 1: 7.
13–14, 17: cf. L 1.1.2.1. For "widened jaws/mouths" cf. Ps. 35: 21, Jb.
16: 10, Lm. 2: 16, 3: 46; for YHWH as a lion, Lm. 3: 10.
15–16 "I am draining away like water, my bones are all disjointed, my heart
is like wax, melting inside me /my strength is drier than a potsherd, and
my tongue is stuck to my jaw (you leave me lying in the dust of death)":
For vv. 15–16 a cf. Ps. 31: 10 b–11, 38: 11, Ez. 37: 11, Lm. 3: 18; for v.
16 b Ps. 137: 6, Ez. 3: 26 (dumbness), Jb. 29: 10 (silence), Lm. 4: 4 (thirst);
v. 16 c is obscure.
18–19 "I can count every one of my bones, and there they glare at me
gloating (/ they divide my garments among them and cast lots for my
clothes)": For v. 18 a cf. Ps. 102: 6, 109: 24, Jb. 7: 15, 19: 20, 33: 21, Lm.
4: 8; for v. 19 cf. Ob. 11–12 ("cast lots", "gloat", "open mouths").

### 1.1.2.3. Ps. 38

7–11 "Bowed down, bent double, overcome, I go mourning all the day /
My loins are burnt up with fever, there is no soundness in my flesh /
numbed and crushed and overcome, my heart groans, I moan aloud /
Lord, all that I long for is known to you, my sighing is no secret from
you / my heart is throbbing, my strength deserting me, the light of my
eyes itself has left me": Ps. 6: 7, 8, 22: 15–16 b, 18 a, 38: 4 a, 39: 4, 102: 4–6,
109: 22 b–23, Is. 1: 6, 21: 3 f., Jr. 45: 3, Jb. 3: 24, 19: 20, 30: 17, 30, Lm.
2: 11, etc. For קדר cf. Ps. 35: 14, 107: 39, Jb. 30: 28.

12 "My friends and companions shrink from my wounds, even the dearest
of them keep their distance": no exact equivalents, cf. however Is. 53: 3.

13 "Men intent on killing me lay snares, others, hoping to hurt me, threaten
my ruin, hatching treacherous plots all day": Ps. 41: 6 ff., 56: 6 f., Jb.
16: 9 f., (Jr. 18: 22), Lm. 3: 61 f. For מבקשי נפשי cf. Ps. 35: 4, 40: 15, 71: 13,
24, for "laying snares/traps" Ps. 119: 110, 140: 6, 142: 4, etc.

### 1.1.2.4. Ps. 69

8–9 "It is for you I am putting up with insults, that cover me with shame /
that make me a stranger to my brothers, an alien to my mother's other
sons": (Jr. 15: 15 ff., 20: 8 f., Jb. 19: 13 ff.).

10 "zeal for your house devours me, and the insults of those who insult
you fall on me": (Ps. 119: 139).

10–13 "If I 'mortify' myself with fasting, they make this a pretext for in-
sulting me / if I dress myself in sackcloth, I become their laughingstock /
the gossip of people sitting at the city gate, and the theme of drunken
songs": (cf. Ps. 44: 16–17 a, 109: 24–25; Jb. 30: 9 ff., Lm. 3: 14, Jr. 24: 9),
for "fasting" cf. Ps. 35: 13, 2 S. 12: 22, 1 K. 21: 27, Neh. 1: 6, for "sackcloth" Ps. 35: 13, Gn. 37: 34, 1 K. 21: 27, Is. 22: 12, Jr. 6: 26, Jon. 3: 6,
Jb. 16: 15, etc.

### 1.1.2.5. Ps. 69

21 "The insults have broken my heart, my shame and disgrace are 'past
cure'; I had hoped for sympathy but in vain, I found no one to console
me": (Lm. 1: 2, 7, 9, 16, 17, 21).

22 "They gave me poison to eat instead, when I was thirsty they gave me
vinegar to drink": Jr. 9: 15, 23: 15, Lm. 3: 15.

### 1.1.2.6. Ps. 88

4–6 "for my soul is all troubled, my life on the brink of Sheol / I am num-
bered among those who go down to the Pit, a man bereft of strength: /
a man alone down among the dead, among the slaughtered in their graves,

among those you have forgotten, those deprived of your protecting hand": Jb. 17: 1, 33: 22. For נגרזו cf. L 1.4.3.

7–8 "You have plunged me to the bottom of the Pit, to its darkest, deepest place / weighted down by your anger, drowned beneath your waves": Jon. 2: 4, (Lm. 3: 6, 54).

9 a–b "You have turned my friends against me and made me repulsive to them": Jb. 19: 13 ff.

9 c–10 a "in prison and unable to escape, my eyes are worn out with suffering": The rendering of v. 9 c is uncertain, for v. 10 a cf. Ps. 6: 8.

## 1.1.2.7. Ps. 88

15 "why do you reject me? Why do you hide your face from me?" Ps. 43: 2, 74: 1, 77: 8 (44: 10, 24, 60: 3, 12, 108: 12, Lm. 3: 17; Ps. 89: 39).

16–18 "Wretched, slowly dying since my youth, I bore your terrors—now I am exhausted / your anger overwhelmed me, you destroyed me with your terrors / which, like a flood, were round me, all day long, all together closing in on me" (Jon. 2: 4, Lm. 3: 6, 54; Jb. 3: 26).

19: cf. v. 9.

## 1.1.2.8. Ps. 102

4–6 "For my days are vanishing like smoke, my bones smouldering like logs / my heart shrivelling like scorched grass, my appetite has gone / whenever I heave a sigh, my bones stick through my skin": Ps. 6: 8, 22: 15–16 b, 18 a, 38: 10 f., 109: 22 b–23, Jr. 45: 3, Ez. 37: 11, Jb. 3: 24, 9: 25 f., 18: 16, 19: 20, 30: 17, 30, 33: 21 f., Lm. 2: 11, 4: 8. For נכה (Po.) cf. Is. 1: 5 f., 53: 4.

7–8 may possibly indicate "forsakenness"—no equivalents of the motif have however been found.

9 "My enemies insult me all day long, those who deride me now use me as a curse": Ps. 44: 16 f., 109: 25, Lm. 3: 16, 61 ff. (cf. also Jr. 24: 9, 25: 9, 18, 42: 17 f., 44: 12).

10 "Ashes are the bread I eat, what I drink I lace with tears": for "ashes" cf. 1 S. 13: 19, Jr. 6: 26, Ez. 27: 30, Jb. 2: 8, 42: 6, Lm. 3: 16.

11 "under your furious anger, since you only picked me up to throw me down": Ps. 22: 16?, 38: 2, 4, 88: 8, 17 f., 89: 47, 90: 7, Jon. 2: 4 (cf. also Jb. 9: 17, 10: 8, 14: 20, 16: 7, 17: 11 ff., 30: ff., etc.).

12 "my days dwindle away like a shadow, I am as dry as hay": Ps. 109: 23, Jb. 9: 25 f., 14: 2, 17: 7 (Ps. 22: 16, Ez. 37: 11, Jb. 18: 16).

## 1.1.2.9. Ps. 109

21–22 "Yahweh, defend me for the sake of your name, rescue me since your love is generous / reduced to weakness and poverty, my heart is wounded": Ps. *69: 17; 25: 16, 40: 18, 69: 30, 86: 1; 55: 1.*

23 "I am dwindling away like a shadow, I am shaken out like a locust": Ps. 102: 12, Jb. 14: 2, 17: 17.

24 "My knees are weak for lack of food, my body thin for lack of oil": Ps. 22: 18 a, 69: 11, 102: 6, Jb. 7: 15, 19: 20, 33: 21, Lm. 4: 8. For צום cf. Ps. 35: 13, 1 S. 12: 22, 1 K. 21: 27, Neh. 1: 6.

25 "I have become an object of derision, people shake their heads at me in scorn": Ps. 31: 12, 44: 14 f., 79: 4, 89: 42, 51, Is. 37: 22, Jr. 18: 16, Ob. 12, Lm. 2: 15, 3: 14, 61 ff.

1.1.3. For a systematization of 1.1.1–1.1.2.9 cf. Appendix III.

1.2.1. A central motif within the substantial, mainly non-formulaic descriptions of misery is "forsakenness"/"ignominy",[3] caused by YHWH or by a third party. In general, a great majority of the realizations of this motif pertain to Israel or parts thereof (Dt. 28: 37, Jr. 24: 9, 29: 18, 44: 8, 12, Ez. 5: 14, 22: 4, Jo. 2: 17 ff., Mi. 6: 6, Ps. 44: 14 ff., 79: 4, 80: 7, 89: 42, 51 a, Dn. 9: 16—cf. also 1 K. 9: 7, Is. 25: 8, 51: 7, 54: 4, Jr. 9: 19, 15: 4, 18: 16, 19: 8, 23: 39 f., 26: 6, 31: 19(18), 42: 18, Ez. 16: 57, 22: 5, 36: 15, Zeph. 3: 18, Lm. 2: 15, 51, Neh. 1: 3, 3: 36, 5: 9), and are, with the exception of Mi. 6: 16, connected with territorial catastrophe or restoration in times to come (for realizations pertaining to individuals in sections not mentioned above cf. Is. 14: 4, Ez. 14: 8, Hab. 2: 6—cf. also Is. 49: 7, 52: 14, 53: 3; for חרפה cf. 1 S. 11: 2, 17: 26, 25: 39, Is. 30: 5, Jr. 6: 10, Hos. 12: 5, Pr. 6: 33, Jb. 19: 5, Dn. 11: 8, 12: 12).

Thus the "forsakenness"/"ignominy"-motif seems to become a literary convention from the time of Jeremiah and onwards, showing its most common applications in references to the condition of the people or parts thereof.

1.2.2. The constitutive elements of Ps. 31: 10–14 recur, isolated or as combinations of motifs, in Ps. 22: 7–11, 12–19, 38: 7–13, 68: 8/9–13, 21–22, 88: 4–10 a, 15–19, 102: 4–12, and 109: (21), 22–25. Outside this group realizations of similar motifs are found in Pss. 6, 39, 41, 43, 44, 56, 60, 71, 74, 77, 79, 89, 90, 108, 119, Jeremiah, Job, and Lamentations; only Ps. 44: 10–17, 89: 39–52, Jr. 15: 15–18, 20: 7–10, Jb. 16: 9–17, 17: 1–7, 30: 9–23, Lm. 3: 1–18/19 do however display combinations of the elements listed. These units may be seen as reflecting a common cultural background, and a literary convention within that background.

1.3. Displaying combinations of subject matter also found in two "national laments",[4] two of the "Confessions" of Jeremiah, two of the "Monologues" of Job, and in "individual" parts of Lm., Pss. 22: 7–11, 12–19, 38: 7–13, 69: 8/9–13, 21–22, 88: 4–10 a, 15–19, 102: 4–12 and 109: 22–25 may be seen as reflecting national or individual distress within a common literary convention.

Whether these sections should be labelled "national" or "individual" must be determined from case to case and against the background of each psalm in its *present* form;[5] only then I shall be in a position to answer the question about the "*actual* application, use and interpretation" (cf. A 2.1) of the units containing substantial non-formulaic accounts of distress.

2. Analyzing Ps. 102 J. Becker (1966: 44) remarks: "Es ist am sinnvollsten, für vv. 2–12 und vv. 24–25 a in ihrem jetzigen kompositionellen Verband eine kollektivierende Neuinterpretation anzunehmen. Die sogenannten sekundären Teile vv. 13–23 und vv. 25 b–29 zeigen an, welcher Art die neue Sinngebung ist: das individuelle Klagelied wird zum Gebet des Volkes im Exil"; furthermore, "Gedanken und Sprache lehnen sich anerkanntermassen stark an deutero – und tritoisaianische Texte an, die ja auch aus derselben heilsgeschichtlichen Situation heraus geschrieben sind" (43). Ps. 69 too displays examples of "Neuinterpretation": "Die Zusätze zeigen an, dass der Redaktor Klage und Dank auf die Situation des Volkes im Exil gedeutet wissen wollte. Das bedeutet nun keineswegs, dass die einzelnen Bilder und Wendungen des Psalmes auf Grund der Neuinterpretation einen neuen Sinn erhalten. Es genügt, dass Klage und Dank als Gesamtheit auf das Volk übertragen werden. Die Einzelheiten werden in allegorischer Form auf das neue Verständnis hingeordnet" (46).

This would imply that the substantial non-formulaic descriptions of distress belong the the "original" material, which, in the course of time, was allegorically applied to the situation of the people. However, as was observed above, such sections conform to a literary convention comprising parts of Jr., Jb., Lm. (cf. also Pss. 44 and 89). Against this background it may be suggested that the redactional activity in exilic/post-exilic times was not limited to eschatological addenda,[6] but also involved specifications of situation within "individual laments", such as Pss. 31, 69 and 102; the motifs, or combinations of motifs, found in these three psalms do however also occur in units not conforming to the compositional convention but displaying thematical homogenity (Pss. 38, 44, 88—cf. also Ps. 89: 39–52) and thus indicating "Neukonzeption" rather than "Neuinterpretation".[7]

2.1.1. In Ps. 31 the "lament" proper was thought to comprise vv. 2 c–9 and 15–18 b (cf. K 4.1.1) with a possible conclusion in vv. 22–23 (cf. חסד in v. 8, 17, 22; הטה אזנך in v. 3 שמעת in v. 23); this "lament" and the account of divine intervention provide a basis of hopefullness for several

115

(vv. 20–21, 24, 25). The form and contents of the plural applications of vv. 20–21, 24, and 25 show similarities to other non-formulaic sections, for which a redactional origin might be suggested, since they follow upon established conclusions and display loose connexions in context (cf. K 3.2, 3.1.6). Becker (1966: 23) states: "Wo (aber) Texte vorkommen, die – im Lichte der formgeschichtlichen Methode – nur auf den Einzelbeter passen, und wo zugleich redaktionelle Anzeichen dafür da sind, dass der Psalm Gebet des Volkes sein soll, bleibt nur die Wahl, Neuinterpretation des Textes anzunehmen. Durch redaktionelle Sinngebung wird der Psalm ausschliesslich Gebet des Volkes, und der individuelle Beter gehört in den Bereich der Vorgeschichte des biblischen Textes."

The situation of the individual, as depicted in v. 5 and referred to in vv. 8–9 is however specified through vv. 10–14. This section contains motifs and combinations of motifs, which within parts of Jr., Jb., Lm. and Pss. 44 and 89 are used to outline national or individual distress.

In the Book of Lamentations, a poetic literature with a fixed date, showing combinations of elements of subject matter similar to those isolated above (1.1.3), "individual lament"-motifs are transmuted into collective usage. N. K. Gottwald (1954: 33 ff.) refers to the national crisis as a cause for the shattering of normal or "typical" forms of speech—type and imagery become subservient to situation and intention; so the author of Lm. "had at his disposal no individual psalms which he incorporated, but only an intimate knowledge of individual lament style. In the high point of his discussion, namely the third poem, he heaps up figures from this individual lament style in order to express the maximum of suffering."[8]

This endeavour to express a "maximum of suffering" may provide the background of the substantial, mainly non-formulaic descriptions of distress (cf. above 1)—if so, Ps. 31: 10–14 does not belong to the "original lament", but is an insertion, reflecting the situation of the nation; exilic/post-exilic "Neuinterpretation" would thus not be limited to plural applications of accounts of salvation but also comprise expositions of the actual cultural background.

2.1.2. In Ps. 69 the "lament"proper was thought to comprise the sections 2–6, 14–16, 17–20, and 30–31; this "lament" and the concluding expressions of confidence provide a basis of hopefulness for several (vv. 33–34, 35–37; cf. K 3.1.6.2).

The situation of the individual, as depicted in vv. 2b–5, and referred to in vv. 15–16 and 17–20, is specified through the non-formulaic sections 8/9–13 and 21–22, stressing the aspect of ignominy. This motif is applied both to individuals and nations (cf. above 1.2.1); in Ps. 69 certain indications disfavour the latter alternative: the distress outlined is not sufficiently all-inclusive[9] and the references to "my brothers" and "my mother's other sons" (v. 9) would be obscure if the whole people of Israel were intended. The cause of the ignominy is however stated as "zeal for your house"— within the cultural background isolated above, this may refer to the propagation for resurrection of the Jerusalem temple and involve individuals or national subgroups and the "Fluch"-section (for the combination distress-"Fluch" cf. Lm. 3: 59–63/64–66) would pertain to the opponents of such a program. If this is correct, Ps. 69: 8/9–13 and 21–22 deal with a problem apparently very acute for the exilic generation(s) and showing a number of literary realizations (cf. Hg. 1, Lm. 2, Ezr. 1 ff., etc.).

These sections show a "Horizont" (cf. above 1.1.2.4–5) that may very well coincide with that outlined for the plural applications of vv. 33–34, 35–37—i.e., the same cultural background might have given raise to expositions of the actual situation within the framework of a traditional "individual lament", and a paradigmatic application of this "lament".[10]

2.1.3. In Ps. 102 the initiating exhortations with motivations show a high density of set phrases (cf. J 1.17), whereas the detailed description of distress is mainly non-formulaic. The "lament" proper is defective, the explanation of which may be sought in the combination of units of different origin (cf. above 2).

In Ps. 31 a former act of salvation provided the basis of confidence for several, in Ps. 102 no such act is accounted for—here the plural applications (vv. 13–23, 25 c–29), initiated by hymnic phraseology, contrast the eternity of YHWH to the transcience of human existence (vv. 4–12).

vv. 4–12 reflect a literary convention within a cultural background which may very well coincide with that outlined for the sections 13–23 and 25 c–29 (cf. K 3.1.6.2), and thus vv. 4–23 and 25 c–29 may be understood as an organic unity. If so, another aspect of exilic thought would be isolated: expanding the references to distress within an "individual lament" with a detailed account of the frailty of human/national (cf. above 2.1.1) existence, the "eternity of YHWH" provides the basis of hope for national restoration (cf. also Is. 51: 6–11, Lm. 3: 19–24).

2.2. Pss. 38, 44, 88 and 89: 39–52 do not conform to the compositional convention, but display motifs similar to those isolated above (cf. 1.1); common to these units is the central problem of forsakenness/ignominy— in Pss. 38, 88, and 89: 32–52 connected with references to YHWH's wrath— and the lack of plural applications.

2.2.1. The introductory exhortations of Ps. 38 form a formulaic system together with Ps. 6: 2 (Culley 1967: no. 81), while the description of situation might be divided into three parts: vv. 3–6, connecting physical suffering with sin and divine wrath (for v. 3 cf. Dt. 32: 23, Jb. 6: 4, 16: 12 f., 27: 22, Lm. 3: 12), vv. 7–13, without such connexions (cf. above 1.1.2.3), and vv. 14–15, outlining the submission of the psalmist (cf. also Is. 53: 7, Jr. 11: 19, Ps. 39: 10, Lm. 3: 30). v. 16 displays terminal traits, but the following motivations contain renewed descriptions of distress and statements seemingly contrary to those of vv. 3–6, rather than the expected modal impfa (cf. K 2.6). This may be explained through the relative frequency of formulaic language within the section 17–23 (cf. v. 18 b, 20 b, 22 a, 22 b, 23 a): i.e., a non-formulaic description of distress, outlining a specific situation, has been supplied with a frame-work (cf. also v. 2) of traditional invocational formulas.

The heaping up of motifs from the "individual lament" style in order to express a "maximum of suffering" (cf. above 2.1.1), the combinations sin–wrath–suffering (forsakenness), and the alphabetic structure indicate an exilic background of Ps. 38—whether the unit pertains to an individual, a subgroup or the nation is however impossible to determine.

2.2.2. In Ps. 44, YHWH's devotion to past generations is contrasted to the situation of the psalmist and his contemporaries (vv. 2–4, 10–17); in spite of confidence and righteousness (vv. 5–9, 18–23), YHWH has abandoned his people, scattered them among the nations, and consigned them to the scorn of their neighbours.

Outside the Book of Job references to ignominy in combination with outright statements of righteousness are very rare—Gunkel (1926: 187) remarks: "Würde der Psalm exilisch sein, so würde man wenigstens die Erinnerung und die Schuld der Vorfahren (II Könige 23, 26, 24, 3 f. Threni 5, 7 u.a.) erwarten dürfen ... Gegenwärtig denkt man meistens ... an die Zeit der Makkabäer, die zuerst wieder ‚Heere' aufgestellt haben, und bezieht dabei den Satz ‚deinethalb werden wir erwürgt' 23 auf die damalige Religionsverfolgung ... ".

If these suppositions as to the origin of Ps. 44 are correct, this would imply that the "ignominy"-motif was not only used to outline the situation of the exilic community, but came to be considered a traditional element in descriptions of national distress.

2.2.3. For Ps. 88 cf. K 5. The heaping up of motifs from the "individual lament" style in order to express a "maximum of suffering" (cf. above 2.1.1, 2.2.1) and the many terminological similarities with the Book of Job (cf. Gunkel, 1926: *ad loc.*) indicate a late time of origin for Ps. 88—whether the unit pertains to an individual, a subgroup, or the nation is however impossible to determine.

2.2.4. In Ps. 89 YHWH's former saving activity and devotion to David and his house are contrasted to the situation of the psalmist and his contemporaries (vv. 2–38, 39–52; cf. Ps. 44: 2–4, 10–17). vv. 39–46 outline the distress of YHWH's anointed, referring not only to ignominy but also to rejection, disownment, repudiation, piercing of all defences, stripping of the crown, etc. in connexion with divine wrath; vv. 47–49 are centered around the "frailty of human existence", while vv. 50–52 specify the situation of Ps. 89—"Lord, where are those earlier signs of your love?"—referring to contemporary ignominy (cf. also Lm. 5: 19–21).

In its present form the unit is to be considered a "national lament"; Gunkel rightly observes: "Die Not, über die das Gedicht klagt, ist nicht ein einzelnes, besonderes Ereignis, sondern die des ganzen Zeitalters", i.e. the period "*nach dem Sturz des judäischen Königtums*" (1926: 396).

2.3. It was suggested above that the "basic lament" of Ps. 109 consists of vv. 1–5, 26–27, and 28–29 (K 3.1.3.1); to these sections vv. 21–25, specifying the situation, and 6–20, outlining the fate desired for the opponents, would have been added, together with the concluding vv. 30–31 (cf. עני ואביון in v. 16, 22, אביון in v. 31). Another interpretation is however possible—if Gottwald's observations that type and imagery become subservient to situation and intention in exilic times (1954: 37) are correct, Ps. 109 may be understood as an organic whole, reflecting a situation of internal confrontation, possibly similar to that outlined in Ps. 69: 8/9–13, 21–22/23–29.

2.4. Ps. 22 displays a concentration of formulaic language in vv. 20–23; as opposed to Ps. 38: 17–23 (cf. above 2.2.1) these stanzas show contents related to other parts of the psalm (for v. 21 cf. v. 17, for v. 22 v. 14, 17), and are thus well integrated in context.

The sections 7–11, focusing on ignominy and confidence, and 12–19, heaping up figures from the "individual lament" style, contain motifs and combinations of motifs which are used to outline national or individual distress within parts of Jr., Pss. 44, 89, Jb. and Lm.; vv. 24–32 show that the account of divine intervention (v. 22 b) has been applied to wider categories.

Becker (1966) suggests that an "individual lament" has been subjected to exilic/post-exilic "Neuinterpretation" (cf. K 3.1.6.2); the "Horizont" outlined for vv. 7–11 and 12–19 may however very well coincide with that of the plural applications (vv. 24–32), and thus it may be argued that

119

Ps. 22 is an exilic "Neukonzeption", where an individual speaks on behalf of the people (cf. v. 5). By combining the themes of suffering and hope the unit aims at conferring trust and confidence in the imminent intervention of YHWH, thereby outlining a new era.

3.1. The *actual* application, use and interpretation of the units containing substantial non-formulaic accounts of distress could only be determined from case to case and against the background of each psalm in its *present* form.

The plural applications in Pss. 22, 31, 69, and 102 indicate that these psalms at one time or other have been interpreted as pertaining to the community or parts thereof; these applications do however show a "Horizont" similar to that outlined for the non-formulaic accounts of distress— these four psalms may thus be seen as reflecting a common cultural background, i.e. that of the exilic/post-exilic community.

In such cases where a basic "individual lament" conforming to the compositional convention (cf. K 4.1.1) was isolated, the non-formulaic plural applications are seen as paradigmatic interpretations of YHWH's intervention or steadfast love accounted for in the lament, while the inserted non-formulaic accounts of distress specify the situation in the community— the particular associations of the "individual lament" offered categories by which this situation could best be described.[11]

The heaping up of motifs from the "individual lament"-style, and the references to wrath–forsakenness suggest an exilic background for Pss. 38 and 88. These units, lacking plural applications, are seen as examples of "Neukonzeption" since they do not conform to the compositional convention; whether they pertain to individuals, subgroups, or the nation is impossible to determine—certain indications, i.e. the existence of "national laments" (Pss. 44, 89: 39–52), displaying similar combinations of motifs and almost certainly of late origin, disfavour the last alternative.

In Ps. 22, also offered as an example of exilic "Neukonzeption", an individual speaks on behalf of the people. The unit is possibly modelled on the "edited" versions of Pss. 31, 69, and 102, and reveals, through the combination of suffering and hope, a basic confidence in the imminent intervention of YHWH.

3.2. The central thoughts in my material are those of suffering and hope, of forsakenness and confidence in the steadfast love of YHWH; the summons to "answer", "listen", not to "desert", "abandon", "reject", or "stand aside" do not only stress the problem of alienation, but show that the conception of YHWH's control of events is still very much alive in Israel's faith.

The message of "Deutero-Isaiah", also centered around suffering and hope, reflects a specific, and probably somewhat later[12] analysis of the situation, the Deuteronomist's work of history displays still another attempt at interpretation—thus the catastrophic events of the fall of Judah led to a considerable theological and literary activity. Only against such a historical background the units containing substantial, non-formulaic descriptions of distress can be understood.

# Appendix I

| Psalm | A Total number of entries in Culley | B "individual complaint"-language compared to the total stock of formulaic language (%) | | C Formulas/formulaic systems and other references in common with Pss. 18–69–86–116 | D The relation between C and A (%) | E Formulas/formulaic systems and other references in common with Pss. 6–25–31–142 | F The relation between E and (%) |
|---|---|---|---|---|---|---|---|
| 6 | 8 | 100 | (8) | 3–5 | 100 | 4–4 | 100 |
| 9 | 13 | 38 | (5) | 1–1 | 15 | 2–1 | 23 |
| 18 | 20 | 75 | (15) | 1–5 | 30 | 1–1 | 10 |
| 22 | 9 | 89 | (8) | 2–1 | 33 | 0–1 | 11 |
| 25 | 8 | 100 | (8) | 4–2 | 75 | 1–4 | 63 |
| 26 | 5 | 60 | (3) | 2–1 | 60 | 1–2 | 60 |
| 27 | 9 | 100 | (9) | 1–1 | 22 | 1–0 | 11 |
| 28 | 8 | 100 | (8) | 1–2 | 38 | 3–4 | 88 |
| 30 | 6 | 67 | (4) | 1–1 | 33 | 2–1 | 50 |
| 31 | 22 | 95 | (21) | 2–5 | 32 | 5–5 | 45 |
| 35 | 13 | 92 | (12) | 1–1 | 15 | 0–2 | 15 |
| 38 | 7 | 100 | (7) | 1–1 | 29 | 1–0 | 14 |
| 40 | 10 | 90 | (9) | 2–1 | 30 | 1–1 | 20 |
| 54 | 5 | 100 | (5) | 0–1 | 20 | 0–1 | 20 |
| 61 | 6 | 100 | (6) | 3–0 | 50 | 1–2 | 50 |
| 69 | 12 | 100 | (12) | 0–5 | 42 | 2–4 | 50 |
| 71 | 15 | 93 | (14) | 1–3 | 27 | 5–3 | 53 |
| 86 | 16 | 81 | (13) | 1–5 | 38 | 6–7 | 81 |
| 88 | 5 | 100 | (5) | 0–4 | 80 | 0–2 | 40 |
| 102 | 8 | 88 | (7) | 2–3 | 63 | 2–0 | 25 |
| 109 | 7 | 100 | (7) | 1–4 | 71 | 3–0 | 43 |
| 116 | 8 | 100 | (8) | 2–5 | 88 | 2–2 | 50 |
| 119 | 10 | 100 | (10) | 2–1 | 30 | 5–0 | 50 |
| 140 | 6 | 100 | (6) | 2–0 | 33 | 2–3 | 83 |
| 142 | 16 | 88 | (14) | 4–2 | 38 | 3–1 | 25 |
| 143 | 20 | 90 | (18) | 2–3 | 25 | 5–6 | 55 |

| A | B | | C | | D | | E | |
|---|---|---|---|---|---|---|---|---|
| Number of formulas/formulaic systems under F–H | Bound in formulas/ formulaic systems with units from the starting group showing similar function in context | | Bound in formulas/ formulaic systems with units outside the starting group | | Differing functionally from other members of the formula/formulaic system | | Bound in formulas/ formulaic systems without common function in context | |
| 9 | 78% | (7) | 22% | (2) | 0% | (0) | 0% | (0) |
| 6 | 17 | (1) | 17 | (1) | 17 | (1) | 50 | (3) |
| 17 | 35 | (6) | 53 | (9) | 0 | (0) | 12 | (2) |
| 9 | 44 | (4) | 11 | (1) | 33 | (3) | 11 | (1) |
| 8 | 25 | (2) | 12.5 | (1) | 50 | (4) | 12.5 | (1) |
| 5 | 0 | (0) | 60 | (3) | 20 | (1) | 20 | (1) |
| 5 | 80 | (4) | 0 | (0) | 20 | (1) | 0 | (0) |
| 6 | 50 | (3) | 50 | (3) | 0 | (0) | 0 | (0) |
| 20 | 55 | (11) | 30 | (6) | 10 | (2) | 5 | (1) |
| 6 | 50 | (3) | 33 | (2) | 17 | (1) | 0 | (1) |
| 6 | 33 | (2) | 33 | (2) | 0 | (0) | 33 | (2) |
| 6 | 33 | (2) | 33 | (2) | 17 | (1) | 17 | (1) |
| 10 | 40 | (4) | 20 | (2) | 0 | (0) | 40 | (4) |
| 14 | 64 | (9) | 18 | (4) | 7 | (1) | 0 | (0) |
| 15 | 73 | (11) | 20 | (3) | 6 | (1) | 0 | (0) |
| 5 | 40 | (2) | 20 | (1) | 40 | (2) | 0 | (0) |
| 8 | 75 | (6) | 25 | (2) | 0 | (0) | 0 | (0) |
| 7 | 14 | (1) | 43 | (3) | 29 | (2) | 14 | (1) |
| 8 | 62.5 | (5) | 0 | (0) | 12.5 | (1) | 25 | (2) |
| 6 | 17 | (1) | 0 | (0) | 33 | (2) | 50 | (3) |
| 14 | 21 | (3) | 29 | (4) | 29 | (4) | 21 | (3) |
| 20 | 40 | (8) | 30 | (6) | 15 | (3) | 15 | (3) |
| 210 | 42.5 | (95) | 27.2 | (57) | 14.2 | (30) | 13.3 | (28) |

# Appendix III

| A<br><br>References to sorrow, physical weakness, etc. | B<br><br>References to forsakenness | C<br><br>References to ignominy | D<br><br>References to plotting or other hostile activity | E<br>References to divine wrath and/or YHWH as originator of distress | F<br><br>Other material |
|---|---|---|---|---|---|
| 31: 10 b–11 | 31: 12 b–13 | 31: 12 a | 31: 14 | – | – |
| – | – | 22: 7–8(9) | – | – | 22: 10–11 |
| 22: 12 b, 15–16 b, 18 a | (22: 12 c) | – | 22: 13–14, 17, 18 b–19 | 22: 16 c(?) | – |
| 38: 7–11 | 38: 12 | – | 38: 13 | – | – |
| 69: 11 a, 12 a | 69: 9 | 69: 10, 11 b, 12 b–13 | (69: 12 b–13) | – | – |
| – | (69: 21 c–d) | 69: 21 a–b | 69: 22 | – | – |
| 88: (4–6), 9 c–10 a | 88: 9 a–b | – | – | 88: 7–8 | – |
| – | 88: (15), 19 | – | – | 88: 16–18 | – |
| 102: 4–6, 10, 12 | 102: 7–8? | 102: 9 | – | 102: 11 | – |
| 109: 22 b–24 | – | 109: 25 | (109: 25) | – | – |
| Ps. 6: 7, 8, 38: 14 a, 39: 4 | | Ps. 44: 14 ff., 79: 4, 89: 42, 51 f. (119: 139) | Ps. 41: 6 ff. (44: 16), 56: 6 f., 71: 10 | Ps. 38: 2, 4, 43: 2 (44: 10), (60: 3, 12), 74: 1, 77: 8 (89: 39), 89: 47, 90: 7 (108: 12) | Ps. 71: 6 |
| Is. 1: 6, 21: 3 f. | | Is. (37: 22) (49: 7) 52: 14, 53: 3 | | | Is. (44: 2, 24) (46: 3) (49: 1 |
| Jr. 9: 18 (14: 17), 45: 3 | Jr. (15: 17) (20: 8 f.) | Jr. 9: 19, 15: 15, 18: 16, 20: 7 f. (24: 9) | Jr. 11: 19 (18: 22), 20: 10 (24: 9) | Jr. (9: 15) (15: 15) (23: 15) | Jr. (1: 5) |
| Ez. 37: 11 | | Ob. (12) | Ob. (11–12) | Jon. 2: 4 | |
| Jb. 3: 24, 7: 15, 9: 25 f., 14: 2, 17: 17, 18: 16, 19: 20, 30: 17, 33: 21 f., 42: 6 | Jb. (19: 13 ff.) | Jb. 16: 20, 17: 2, 6, 30: 9 | Jb. 16: 9, 10 (30: 9 ff.) | Jb. 19: 13 ff. (9: 17, 10: 8, 14: 20, 16: 7, 17: 11, 30: 20 ff., etc.) | |
| Lm. (1: 11), 2: 11, 3: 18 (3: 54), 4: 8, 5: 17 | Lm. 1: 7 (1: 2, 9, 16, 17, 21) | Lm. 2: 15, 3: 14, 16, 61 ff. (5: 1) | Lm. 3: 60 ff. | Lm. 3: 6, 54 (3: 17) | |
| | | Dn. (9: 16) | | | |

# NOTES

## Chapter A

1. Johnson (1955: 104).
2. (1962: 1484 ff.).
3. (1945: 33).
4. (1955: 56).
5. Ringgren (1967: 63 f.).
6. Ibid. (1966: 235 f.).
7. Ibid. (1967: 64).

## Chapter B

1. Richter (1971: 75 ff.).
2. Ibid. (77 f.).
3. Ibid. (102 f.). Cf. below C.

## Chapter C

1. Richter (1971: 78).
2. Ibid. (1971: 117).
3. Richter (1971: 103).
4. Ibid. (1971: 103, 102).

## Chapter D

1. For a description of Parry's works cf. preface and introduction to Lord (1954) and Levin (1937: 259–266).
2. Cf. foreword to Lord (1965). For other studies based on the works of Parry and Lord cf. Culley (1967: Appendix).
3. Cf. Culley (1963: 113–125), (1976: 15–19).
4. For the discussion on "formularity" cf. Wittig (1976: 66 ff.), Coote (1976: 53 ff.).
5. With Coote (1976: 54 f.): "Culley, who confesses no special insight into the mysteries of Hebrew meter (1970), is thus guided by the repeated whole phrases that he finds into describing the metrical parameter in the definition of the Hebrew formula as the length of the verse line. Culley's description of the Hebrew formula is inductive, based on the full use of repeated phrases and lines in the Psalms, extendible to other bodies of biblical poetry, and probably irrefutable. It is an important discovery."
6. Cf. Richter (1971: 78).
7. Wittig (1976: 84, n. 3) distinguishes between *text description, text presentation* and *text generation;* the first of these involves "the critical act of counting formulas, ascertaining

the limits of formula systems within a given text, outlining motif- and scene-patterns and so on".

In order not to be accused of the "general failure to view the poetic work as a composite whole, to integrate the stylistic particles that make up the linguistic surface of the work with larger formulaic structures or agglomerations of structures" (Ibid., 68) I shall stress the context analysis and the investigation of function in context.

This is, however, only a first and necessary step to avoid subjectivity (cf. B), and should provide a basis for "searching out those recurring associative features that provide the latent structure and attempting to see the a-temporal, deep-structure organization beneath the temporal organization imposed on the work's surface". (Ibid., 82)

As for text generation, I would ask which structuring patterns are obligatory and which are arbitrary. To answer this question I think an analysis of the formulaic language might be helpful. The question of text generation will be treated in the latter part of the investigation.

8. Culley (1967: 10).

9. Ibid. (1967: 12).

10. For a survey of the theories cf. Eissfeldt (1964: 75 ff.), Mowinckel (1962: II, 261–266), Kosmala (1964: 423 ff.).

11. Culley (1967: 29 f.).

12. Ibid. (1967: 30).

13. "Since the complaints and thanksgivings are so closely related and have a great deal of subject matter in common, they could be considered one group as far as common language is concerned." Culley (1967: 103).

14. This group also includes Ps. 144 with seven instances of formulaic language—these, however, refer to one single psalm, 18, and include much doubtful material—and Ps. 89 with six instances, all of them more or less doubtful variants. Pss. 144 and 89 will not be included in the main group of "formulaic psalms".

# Chapter E

1. Psalm 18 has the term "ebed" only in the heading, but shows 20 entries in Culley's index and has therefore been judged as suitable for the first control group.

2. Culley (1967: 91), no. 176.

3. Ibid. (49), no. 27.

4. Ibid. (40f.), no. 10.

5. Ibid. (41), no. 10.

6. Ibid. (90), no. 172.

7. Ibid. (90), no. 174.

8. Ibid. (42), no. 14.

9. Ibid. (89), no. 171.

10. Ibid. (48), no. 26.

11. Ibid. (48), no. 26.

12. Ibid. (51), no. 32.

13. Ibid. (43), no. 16.

14. Ibid. (46), no. 21.

15. Ibid. (50, 45): The constant part of the phrase amounts to about half a colon. This is one of the systems suggesting that formal divisions smaller than the colon occasionally

appear so that the colon may be viewed as being composed of two units about half a colon long.

16. Cf. above n. 15.
17. Culley (1967: 51), no. 32.
18. Ibid. (35 f.) no. 1.
19. Ibid. (44): The basic pattern of an imperative followed by a noun with a suffix may serve as a colon itself without any additions, but often such a short phrase can be expanded by a DN or another noun. In the present case, the extra element varies from a conjunction followed by an imperative with suffix in 25: 20 to a clause in 86: 2—the phrase is expanded by an extra element in 6: 5 and 116: 4.
20. Ibid. (43), no. 16.
21. Ibid. (39f.), no. 8.
22. Ibid. (66), no. 64.
23. Ibid. (61 f.), no. 55.
24. Cf. *comm. ad.* 86: 1 a.
25. Culley (49), no. 27.
26. Cf. *comm. ad.* 86: 2 a.
27. Cf. Appendix I, Table B.
28. Ps. 13 1+1, 43 1+1, 47 1+0, 50 1+0, 55 1+0, 57 1+1, 59 0+1, 63 0+1, 66 0+1, 77 1+0, 79 0+1, 91 0+1, 94 0+1, 97 2+0, 103 1+0, 104 1+0, 111 1+1, 120 1+1, 123 0+1, 138 1+1, 139 0+1, 145 2+0 (the first number refers to registered formulas and formulaic systems, the second to more uncertain references).
29. From Ps. 86: 1 a to 17: 6 c, 86: 2 a–17: 13 d, 116: 2 a–17: 6 d, 116: 4 b–17: 13 d.
30. From Ps. 69: 17 a to 56: 2 a, 86: 3 a–56: 2 a, 86: 13 b–56: 14 a, 116: 8 a–56: 14 a, 116: 8 f–56: 14.
31. Cf. Appendix I, Table D.
32. Ps. 18 was part of the first control group, and could have been subject to distorted registration. Further investigation will determine whether the psalm is to belong to a certain group with common formulaic language.
33. Cf. Appendix I, Table A.
34. Culley (1967: 76, 45, 44).
35. Ibid. (54 f.), no. 40.
36. Ibid. (40), no. 9.
37. Ibid. (53), no. 37.
38. Ibid. (52), no. 34.
39. Ibid. (44), no. 17.
40. Ibid. (53), no. 37.
41. Ibid. (53), no. 37.
42. Ibid. (44), no. 18.
43. Ibid. (35f.), no. 1.
44. Ibid. (51), no. 33.
45. Ibid. (42), no. 14.
46. Ibid. (58), no. 47.
47. Ibid. (57), no. 45.
48. Ibid. (38), no. 6.
49. Ibid. (39) no. 7.
50. Ibid. (50), no. 29.
51. Ibid. (51), no. 32.
52. Ibid. (39f.), no. 8.

53. Ibid. (56), no. 43.
54. Cf. Appendix I, Table F.
55. Ps. 142 was part of the second control group, cf. *comm. ad.* n. E 32.
56. Cf. Culley (1967: 38).
57. Ps. 3 2+0, 32 1+0, 36 0+1, 43 2+0, 55 0+1, 57 0+1, 63 1+0, 66 1+1, 77 2+0, 79 1+0, 80 1+0, 83 1+0, 90 1+1, 118 1+0, 120 1+1, 123 0+1, 139 1+0.
58. From Ps. 25: 2 a–b to 16: 1, 25: 20 b–c–16: 1, 31: 2 a–b–16: 1, 31: 15 b–c–16: 2 a–b, 142: 6 b–16: 2 a.
59. From Ps. 6: 5 a to 17: 13 d, 25: 20 a–b–17: 13 d, 31: 3 a–17: 6 c, 31: 21 a–17: 8 b.
60. From Ps. 6: 3 to 56: 2 a, 6: 3 c–56: 2 a, 31: 10 a–56: 2 a.
61. Notwithstanding these criteria Ps. 22 will be kept in the investigation as the psalm has played a very important role in the traditional exegesis of "Ebed YHWH"-psalms.
62. Cf. Culley (1967: 53, 51).

# Chapter F

1. Richter (1971: 101).
2. Culley (1967: 50 f.), no. 31.
3. Ps. 86 is structured through the expressions of confidence in v. 5, 8, 10, 13, 15 and 17 c. With the exception of v. 13 b and 17 c these are nominal, and describe YHWH's nature; v. 13 and 17 c deal with the relation between YHWH and the psalmist.
The psalm is divided into the following sections (in this case, as in the following descriptions of structure, the "headings" will not be taken into account):
vv. 1–5, where exhortations precede motivations constructed with ki and nominal clauses (v. 1 c, 2 b) or (iterative) impfa 1 sg (v. 3 b, 4 b: cf. Michel, 1960: § 24, 1). The nominal clause in v. 5 does not directly relate to an exhortation, and is seen as a motivation for the whole section.
vv. 6–8, initiated by two adjacent clauses in the imperative (v. 6 a, 6 b), followed by a description of the invocational situation (impf 1 sg קרא—cf. Ps. 18: 7, 22: 3, 28: 1, 30: 9, 86: 3, etc.) and ki with impf 2 sg (cf. Ps. 17: 6, 142: 8). The nominal clauses in v. 8 lack the initial ki which is found in v. 5, 10, 13 and 17 c.
vv. 9–10, lacking clauses in the imperative and first person sing references—here the relation between YHWH and a third party is described (perf 2 sg–impf 3 pl×3).
vv. 11–13, initiated by an exhortation (v. 11 a), followed by modal impfa 1 sg (v. 11 b–12—note the repetition of שם in 11 b, 12 b), and motivating expressions of confidence (cf. above).
vv. 14–15, initiated by a vocative, followed by perf 3pl×3; v. 15 is initiated by waw.
vv. 16–17 contain five exhortations, followed by impf 3pl×2 and ki with perf 2 sg.
4. According to Culley's index (1967: 36, 44) v. 1 a and 2 a are followed by an x-element.
5. Ps. 109 is divided into the following sections:
vv. 1–5, initiated by a negative command (v. 1), followed by a detailed, motivating account of the activities of a hostile third party (vv. 2–5, mainly in perf–impf cons 3 pl).
vv. 6–20, also initiated by an exhortation (v. 6 a), followed by modal impfa (vv. 6 b–20) with motivations in vv. 16–18 (perf 3sg–impf cons 3 pl). v. 19 is a thematic continuation of the previous stanza and contains modal impfa, v. 20 forms the conclusion of the section. With the exception of v. 20 the unit lacks first person sing references.
vv. 21–25 (26–27), where the first exhortation is followed by a motivating, nominal ki-clause. The second, following the same pattern as the first in turn introduces a detailed description of misery (vv. 22 b–25, in the perfect).

vv. 26–27 contain two exhortations followed by impfa 3 pl and <u>ki</u> with a nominal clause. The section is closed by perf 2 sg.

vv. 28–29, which have been combined chiefly on the ground of similar contents—the section describes the contrasts between an (undefined) third party on the one hand and YHWH and the psalmist on the other.

v. 30, characterized by modal impfa 1 sg.

v. 31, appearing to motivate the preceding stanza (<u>ki</u> and impf 3 sg), but lacking first person sing references.

6. With the exception of v. 1, most of the stanzas of Ps. 25 belong thematically together in pairs (cf. v. 2f., 4f., 6f., 8f., 12f., 14f.). v. 1 is regarded as a description of the invocational situation—as such it constitutes the background of the following statements.

vv. 2–3 reflect confidence and point terminologically to v. 20b. Michel (1960: § 23,4) stresses the modal aspect of the impfa of v. 3.

vv. 4–15 show a relatively uniform terminology—so דרך appears in v. 4, 8, 9, 12; הודיע in v. 4, 14; ארח in v. 4, 10; למד in v. 4, 5, 9; דרך (Hiph.) in v. 5, 9; ירה (Hiph.) in v. 8, 12 and טוב in v. 8 and 13. The section 4–7 is characterized by exhortations with first person sing suffixes; vv. 8–11 and 12–15 do not pertain directly to the psalmist but contain first person sing references at the end of each subsection (v. 11, 15).

vv. 16–20b (20c–21, 22) contain exhortations and motivations—the latter pertain to the character, activities, or situation of the psalmist.

v. 20c–21 contain expressions of confidence (neg impf 1 sg) with <u>ki</u> and perf 1 sg, impf 3 pl with <u>ki</u> and perf 1 sg) and form the actual conclusion of the psalm, since v. 22 breaks the acrostic pattern and deviates, as far as contents are concerned, from the rest of the unit.

7. Ps. 69 is divided into the following sections:

vv. 2–6, introduced by an exhortation, which is motivated from different aspects (vv. 2b–3 water/mire, v. 4 lengthy invocation, v. 5 hostile third party, v. 6 YHWH's familiarity with the psalmist) in the form of verbal clauses in the perfect.

vv. 7–8, introducing a third party with special relations to YHWH and the psalmist (v. 7— cf. the suffixes) and showing divine names unknown in the rest of the psalm (אלהי ישראל /אדני יהוה צבאות).—v. 8 seems to motivate the exhortations of the preceding stanza (<u>ki</u> and perf).

vv. 9–13, containing a description of misery (vv. 9–12 in perf–impf cons; v. 13, explaining the reactions of the surrounding people, in impf 3 pl with first person sing object).

vv. 14–16, initiated by a description of invocation (v. 14a), followed by exhortations with references to YHWH's attributes, to water/mire and to a hostile third party (vv. 14b–15). v. 16 develops the water-motif and contains triple negative commands without motivations.

vv. 17–20, containing exhortations with motivations referring to YHWH's attributes, and to the (miserable) situation of the psalmist (vv. 17–19). v. 20 stresses YHWH's familiarity with the psalmist.

vv. 21–22, initiated by a short account of misery (perf), followed by references to the reactions and activities of the psalmist (impf cons×2), and to the reactions of the surrounding people (impf cons 3 pl with first person sing object).

vv. 23–29, displaying wishes concerning a third party—with the exception of v. 27 without motivations. The section lacks first pers sing references.

v. 30, initiated by <u>wa'ani</u> (cf. v. 14) referring to the character of the psalmist, and containing a wish concerning divine protection (modal impf 2 s–s1 sg).

vv. 31, 32, which may be seen as the continuation of v. 30, or interpreted as independent units. The latter alternative is favoured by the fact that modal impfa 2/3 sg are not usually followed by cohortatives in conclusions within the starting group (cf. K 2.6); v. 32 lacks first person sing references.

vv. 33–34, initiated by perf 3 pl (33 a), followed by modal impfa 3 pl. For v. 33 a cf. *app. crit.* BHS *ad loc.* The section lacks first person sing references.

vv. 35–37, initiated by an exhortation, addressed to a plural category, followed by motivations (ki and impf 3 sg) and impfa 3 pl. The section lacks first person sing references and differs, as far as contents are concerned, from the rest of the psalm.

8. Culley (1967: 74), no. 97.

9. Ps. 116 is divided into the following sections:

vv. 1–2, combined mainly because of similar contents (הטה אזן-ישמע). The question of aspect presents certain problems; ki with impf 2sg is unusual (cf. however Ps. 17: 6, 86: 7, 142: 8). The text seems to be corrupt.

vv. 3 a–b, describing a situation of distress (perf 3pl–s1sg).

vv. 3 c–4, outlining the invocational situation (vv. 3 c–4 a; impfa 1sg) and introducing an exhortation.

vv. 7–8, initiated by an imperative, followed by motivations (ki and perf 3sg, perf 2sg).

v. 9, with modal impf 1sg.

vv. 10–11, containing a presentation of the psalmist (vv. 10 a–b), and a description of situation (vv. 10 c–11). The verbal clause of v. 11 a seems to introduce a quotation (cf. F 1.3.1, 2.1.2).

vv. 12–14, initiated by a question (v. 12), which is answered by describing the actions of the psalmist (vv. 13–14; impfa 1sg).

v. 15, containing a nominal clause without references to the first person sing. The stanza stands isolated in context.

vv. 16 a–c seem to contain another presentation (cf. vv. 10 a–b); v. 16 d reports YHWH's saving activity (perf 2sg).

For vv. 17–18 cf. vv. 13–14; v. 19 locates the activities described in the preceding section.

LXX and Hier have "novum Ps." from v. 10, but this supposition is not necessary: vv. 3–9 show several "individual lament"-traits and contain formulaic language in v. 2 a, 3 a–b, 4 b–c, 7 b and 8 a, while vv. 10–19 only show two set phrases (v. 11 a, 16 b), focus on the activities of the psalmist (אזבח × 2, אשלם × 2, אקרא /אשא /אשיב /אמרתי /אדבר) and state certain localities (v. 14 b, 18 b, 19)—against this background I find that vv. 10–19 contain the practical, personal consequences of the salvation described in vv. 7 b–8; the psalm is thus a thematical unit (cf. מות in v. 3—המותה in v. 15, אנה יהוה in v. 4, 16, גמל in v. 7—תגמולהי in v. 12 and ובשם יהוה אקרא in v. 4 a, 13 b, 17 b)—vv. 1–2 form the summarizing heading of this unit.

10. v. 16 might be combined with vv. 17–18 to form a section, which would show certain similarities to vv. 10–11/12–14, both of them starting with a presentation of the psalmist (vv. 10–11, 16 a–c), followed by a reference to YHWH's intervention (v. 12 b, 16 d) and the actions of the delivered (vv. 13–14, 17–18).

11. Cf. Nyberg (1952: §§ 95 g, anm.; 97 f.).

12. Ps. 143 is divided into the following sections:

vv. 1–4, containing exhortations (v. 1 a, 1 b, 1 c, 2 a) and motivations initiated by ki. The first of these is impersonal (v. 2 b; impf 3sg), the second, divided into two parts, describes the activities of a third party (v. 3; perf), and the state of the psalmist (v. 4; impf).

vv. 5–6, describing a situation and containing, with the exception of v. 5 c, perfa 1sg.

vv. 7–10 b, dominated by exhortations, which are motivated by verbal clauses in the perfect with (v. 8 a, 8 d), or without (v. 7 b, 7 d, 9 b) an initiating ki, and finally by a nominal clause (v. 10 b). The exhortations in v. 8 c and 10 a show contents differing from those of v. 7 a, 7 c, 8 a and 9 a in that they belong to an "instruction" category.

vv. 10c–12 contain modal impfa, preceded by nouns with prepositions (v. 10c excluded) and second person sing suffixes (vv. 10c–12a), leading into perf cons (v. 12b) and a motivation (v. 12c; ki with nominal clause).

13. Culley (1967: 50), no. 29. Under this heading I deal only with nominal clauses, so that Ps. 143: 3 will be disregarded for the time being.

14. Ps. 142 is divided into the following sections:

vv. 2–4b, describing the invocational situation (vv. 2–4a; impf 1sg of *verba cordis,* and a nominal clause) and introducing an expression of confidence (v. 4b in the perf; cf. also Ps. 31: 8, 69: 6, 139: 2, 4, 40: 10).

vv. 4c–5, containing an account of distress—a hostile third party is introduced (perf 3pl)—followed by summons to YHWH to observe a state of need.

v. 6 contains *verba cordis* in the *perfect.* The stanza seems to form a transition between the account of distress and the following exhortations, in that it quotes utterances of the psalmist in a specific situation (cf. F 1.3.1.1 and 2.1.2).

vv. 7–8, dominated by exhortations, in v. 7a and 7c motivated by ki and perf, in v. 8 followed by a preposition and inf constr. vv. 8c–d represent something of a problem—I follow Michel's interpretation (1960: § 36, 33) and read v. 8 as modal (for ki and impf 2/3sg cf. Ps. 17: 6, 69: 36, 86: 7, 109: 31, 116: 1, 140: 13).

15. Jon. 2 was not included in the starting group, but since vv. 3–10 contain eight instances of formulaic language and also show motif-similarities to psalms within that group, the unit defends a place in the investigation. Jon 2: 3–10 is divided into the following sections:

| vv. 3a–b | invocation, answer | A | perf 1sg–impfcons 2sg |
| c–d | | | perf 1 sg–perf 2sg |
| v. 4a | changed situation | B | impfcons 2sg |
| vv. 4b–c | distress | C | impf 3sg–perf 3pl |
| v. 5 | problem | D | perf 1sg–impf 1sg |
| vv. 6–7b | distress | C | impf 3sg–perf 1sg |
| v. 7c | changed situation | B | impfcons 2sg |
| v. 8 | invocation, answer | A | perf 1sg–impfcons 3sg |
| v. 9 | wish | E | impf 3pl |
| v. 10 | promise | F | impf 1sgx2 |

16. Culley (1967: 50), no. 30.

17. In Ps. 31 exhortations in the singular are present in vv. 2–3, 10, in the plural in v. 24, 25. vv. 2c–3 are motivated by ki and a nominal clause (v. 4a), followed by modal impfa and ki with a nominal clause (vv. 4b–5); v. 10a is motivated by ki and a nominal clause (v. 10b), leading into a description of misery (10c–14, in the perfect)—the exhortations of v. 24 and 25 lack motivations. Tentatively I divide the psalm into the following sections:

vv. 2a/c–5, introduced by expressions of confidence in perf 1sg and neg impf 1sg (vv. 2a–b, cf. Ps. 71: 1), followed by four exhortations with motivation and three modal impfa with motivation (cf. above).

vv. 6–7, introduced by impf 1sg, but otherwise containing perfa 1sg. v. 6a might be seen as iterative; the whole section expresses confidence.

vv. 8–9, introduced by two cohortatives with second person sing object, introducing motivations ('asher and perf 2sg with first person sing object).

For vv. 10–14 cf. above.

vv. 15–18b (18c–19) addressing YHWH. The terminological similarities to vv. 2–9 should be noted: v. 15a refers back to v. 7b, 16a to 6a, 16b to 3b and 9a, 17b to 3d, and 18a to 2b.

vv. 18c–19 contain no such similarities to preceding sections—the section also lacks a direct address to YHWH.

vv. 20–21, addressing YHWH but lacking first person sing references. v. 20 contains perfa, v. 21 impfa—the two are brought together because of similar contents.

v. 22, 23, initiated by a "bārūk"-statement, followed by ki and perf 3sg (cf. Ps. 28:6). The latter part of v. 22 seems to describe a situation, as does v. 23a, which also contains אמרתי, indicating a quotation (cf. F 1.3.1.1, 2.1.2); this quotation presents perf 1sg (v. 23b), followed by a reference to YHWH's hearing (i.e. the petitions—v. 23c) and another indication of situation (v. 23d). Whether or not these two stanzas originally belong together is left open. For vv. 24, 25 cf. above.

Thus the psalm contains two lengthy sections introduced by exhortations, i.e. vv. 2–9 and 10–18b. The exhortations of vv. 2c–3 are followed by expressions of confidence and modal impfa 1sg with motivations, while v. 10a introduces a description of misery (vv. 10b–14); vv. 2–9 and 15–19b show terminological similarities, vv. 18c–19, 20–21, 24 and 25 lack first person sing references.

18. Culley (1967:72), no. 87.

19. Ibid. (73), no. 95.

20. Phrases in which different parts of the body stand as equivalents for the personality will also be included under this heading.

21. Culley (1967:57), no. 45. Note however that Ps. 116:11 lacks the initial copula.

22. Ps. 30 is divided into the following sections:

vv. 2–4, initiated by modal impf 1sg–s2sg, followed by ki and perf 2sg–s1sg and neg perf 2sg (v. 2)—a construction otherwise common in conclusions (cf. K 2.6). v. 3 contains perf 1sg and impfcons 2sg–s1sg describing an act of invocation and its consequences—v. 4 develops this theme (perf 2sg×2).

vv. 5–6, initiated by two exhortations in the plural (v. 5a, 5b), followed by ki and a nominal clause (v. 6a), and further by a verbal clause in the impf (v. 6b). The section lacks first person sing references.

vv. 9–13, showing several traits common to units within the starting group: account of invocational situation (v. 9; impf 1sg קרא—cf. Ps. 18:7a–b, 28:1a, 116:4a, 142:2), motivations for YHWH's support (v. 10—more common are, however, direct motivations with references to enemies or misery), exhortations (v. 11) followed by perf 2/3sg (v. 12), and modal impfa (v. 13; cf. Ps. 22:20–24, 109:26–27, 116:7–9).

Some terminological similarities are present between vv. 2–6 and 9–13; thus זמר appears in v. 5 and 13, ידה in v. 5 and 13. Cf. also ירד in v. 4 and 10, שאול/בור in v. 4 and 10, although the "death"-motif is seen from different aspects in these two stanzas—v. 4 underlines the saving activity, v. 10 poses a question. This balance between "certainty"–"uncertainty" is also found within vv. 7–8—Michel (1960:§7, 15) notices that the use of tenses differ from that of "individual laments" and includes the section in a description of misery. This is done from a predeterminated "Gattungsbestimmung" (cf. also §10, 12). I prefer to try to let the analysis determine the genre of the psalm, rather than vice versa, so I tentatively suggest that vv. 7–8 are a transition between the sections 2–6 and 9–13 on the grounds stated above.

23. Is. 38:10–20 was not included in the starting group, but as the unit plays an important role in Ringgren's argumentation for "royal passion"—or "Ebed YHWH"-psalms (cf. A 4) it is worth a place in the investigation.

"The psalm of Hezekiah" presents almost as many interpretations (and emendations) as there are commentators on the text. Concerning vv. 15–16 in particular the confusion seems to be almost total, while the exegesis of vv. 10–14 and 17 presents a certain amount of agreement: the former are seen as a lament, introducing an exhortation, the latter as an account of salvation. I shall not present still another interpretation of the unit, but prefer to follow H. S. Nyberg (1973). His structuring runs as follows:

| | |
|---|---|
| vv. 10–12 d: | "Klage in Todesnot" |
| vv. 12 e–14 b: | "Die Gottesverlassenheit" |
| vv. 14 c–15: | "Zaghafte Hinwendung zu Gott" |
| v. 16: | "Das Gebet" |
| v. 17: | "Das Heil durch Leiden und Sündenvergebung" |
| vv. 18–19: | "Danksagung des Dichters" |
| (v. 20: | "Liturgischer Abschluss") |

24. Culley (1967: 73), no. 96.
25. Ibid. (72), no. 88.
26. Ps. 6 is divided into the following sections:
vv. 2–6, characterized by exhortations (v. 2a, 2b, 3a, 5a, 5b, 5c) and motivations (v. 3b, 3d–4a). The negative commands of v. 2 are not motivated, the exhortations of v. 3 are followed by $ki$ and references to the condition of the psalmist (perfa) and a question, addressed to YHWH, the summons of v. 5 are followed by l$^e$ma'an and n-s2sg. v. 6 is not directly preceded by an exhortation and lacks first person sing references—the stanza is seen as a motivation to the whole section (cf. Ps. 86: 5).
vv. 7–8 describing the situation of the psalmist. For the perfind and impfind cf. Nyberg (1952: § 86 n,o).
vv. 9–11 (9–10a, 10b–11) initiated by an exhortation in the plural, motivated by $ki$ and perf 3sg (v. 9b)—the perf 3sg recurs in v. 10a, while v. 10b contains impf 3sg and, compared to v. 10a, inverted wordorder. Michel (1960: § 7, 4) comments: "Die beiden perfa. vv. 9b–10a berichten deutlich Fakten, die der Dichter gerade erlebt hat ... In v. 11 werden die impfa. allgemein modal verstanden ... und man wird dieser Deutung zustimmen. Die impfa. berichten also keine geschehenen Fakten, sondern bezeichnen ein Eintreten ... Das Nächstliegende ist nun, das impf. v. 10b ebenfalls modal zu verstehen."
27. Culley (1967: 74), no. 98.
28. Ibid. (72), no. 89.
29. Ibid. (72), no. 90.
30. Ps. 102 is divided into the following sections:
vv. 2–4/5–12, where v. 2a, 2b, 3a, 3c and 3d contain exhortations (for the close relationship between imperative and jussive, cf. Gesenius, 1910: §§ 46, 48), which are motivated in v. 4 ($ki$ and perf 3pl×2).
vv. 5–12 constitute a detailed description of misery (with the exception of v. 12 in perf–impf cons). The terminological similarities between v. 5 and 12 should be noted.
vv. 13/14–23, lacking references to the first person. The section, which is initiated by hymnic phraseology, shows contents differing from those of the preceding section—in vv. 14–23 the relations between YHWH–Zion–the peoples are considered.
v. 24 is textually problematic but deals with the relation between a third person and the psalmist, while v. 25 addresses YHWH. v. 24b and 25b contain the term ימי, which is also found in v. 4a and 12a; v. 25c seems to be terminologically related to the sections 13/14–23 and 26–29 (דר in v. 13, 19, 25, שנותיך in v. 25, 28). vv. 26–29, lacking first person sing references. The section is initiated by hymnic phraseology.

133

31. Culley (1967: 72), no. 91.

32. Ibid. (57 f.), no. 46.

33. Ibid. (75), no. 102.

34. Ibid. (75), no. 107.

35. Ibid. (67), no. 65. Only 142:4 and 143:8 contain first person sing forms. The expression is found in the former part of 142:4a and in the latter part of 143:8c.

36. Nouns with second person sing suffixes, referring to YHWH, as objects will also be included under this heading.

37. Culley (1967: 53), no. 37.

38. Ps. 71 is divided into the following sections:

vv. 2–5, containing exhortations (for the relation imperative–jussive cf. above n. F 30) in v. 2a, 2b, 2c, 2d, 3a, 4a, motivated in v. 3d and 5a–b by ki with nominal clauses, containing expressions of confidence.

vv. 6–8, with perf 1sg (v. 6a, 7a) and nominal clauses, containing expressions of confidence (v. 6b, 6c, 7c), leading into modal impf (v. 8).

vv. 9–11, 12–13 introduced by negative commands (v. 9), motivated by a description of the activities of a hostile third party (v. 10, perf 3pl), and a direct quotation of utterances directed toward the psalmist (perf 3sg-s, impf–modal impf-s), followed by a motivation. Against this background the commands of v. 12 should be interpreted; v. 13 contains modal impfa referring to a third party (cf. שטני נפשי in v. 13—שמרי נפשי in v. 9).

vv. 14–15, 16–19a contain several nouns with second pers sing suffixes (v. 14a, 15a, 15b, 16b, 17b, 18d, 19a). The section is opened by waw with pronoun preceding the impf–perf cons 1sg; v. 16, on the same theme, has modal impf, motivated by ki and perf 1sg.

v. 16 contains a new start—the two modal impfa are followed by perf 2sg-s (v. 17a) as a sort of motivation—which, in turn, gives the next modal impf (v. 17b; cf. min-weʿad). The ʿad of v. 17b points forward to v. 18a, followed by a negative command and another "ʿad-clause", picking up the verb from v. 17b; v. 19 is a direct continuation of the preceding stanza. vv. 16–19 could perhaps be designated a "link-composition". Along with the above-mentioned nouns the section is held together by verbs of similar content (נגד, ספר, זכר).

vv. 19–20b show hymnic traits and indications of plural suffixes while

vv. 20c–21 have singular suffixes. Common to both is תשוב with impf 2sg(-s).

vv. 22–24a are modal and contain statements of praise. There are, however, certain formal differences within the section: v. 22 contains modal impfa 1sg and is initiated by adv pr (1sg), while vv. 23–24a have impf 3sg–perf 2sg–impf 3sg (cf. v. 15a). Furthermore, in vv. 22 YHWH is addressed with אלהי and קדוש ישראל, while vv. 23–24a lack such epithets.

v. 24b, being, as far as contents are concerned, parallel to v. 13. Note, however, the differences in aspect between the two.

vv. 2–5, 9–11 and 12–13 contain exhortations and references to a hostile third party, v. 13 shows terminal traits (cf. G 5.4.2.1). The sections in between contain expressions of confidence and praise (vv. 6–8, 14–19a, 23–24) and recurrent terminology (צדק in v. 15a, 16b, 19a, 24a, כל היום in v. 8b, 15b, 24a and תהלה in v. 6c, 8a and 14a—cf. also פי in v. 8a, 15a—שפת in v. 23a); vv. 19–20b show form and contents differing from the rest of the psalm, vv. 20c–21 are terminologically related to vv. 19b–20b.

v. 1 is seen as the heading to the psalm in its present form, vv. 24b–c as the conclusion.

39. Culley (1967: 51) no. 33.

40. Ps. 140 is divided into the following sections:

vv. 2–4 initiated by exhortations (v. 2a, 2b) with first person sing suffixes; the third party mentioned in v. 2 is qualified in vv. 3–4 (ʾasher and perf 3pl–impf 3pl, perf 3pl).

134

vv. 5–6, initiated by exhortations (v. 5a, 5b) with first person sing suffixes; the third party mentioned in v. 5a–b is qualified in vv. 5c–6 ($^a$sher and perf 3pl×4), and their activities against the psalmist are underlined.

vv. 7–8, initiated by an "āmarti"-phrase (cf. also F 1.3.1.1), followed by an exhortation with first person sing object (v. 7b); v. 8a is a nominal clause, containing an expression of confidence, v. 8b is verbal (perf 2sg) with first person sing object.

vv. 9–12 are textually corrupt, but seem to contain wishes concerning a third party (neg impf×2 in v. 9, modal impfa in vv. 10–12)—the terminology from the sections 2–4 and 5–6 recurs there. With the exception of v. 10a references to the first person are lacking.

v. 13 opens with perf 1sg, followed by _ki_ and impf 3sg (cf. _comm. ad_ 116: 1) and expresses confidence.

v. 14 has modal impfa 3pl and second person sing object.

41. The initiating _waw_ is seen as expressing emphasis.

42. Culley (1967: 74), no. 98 c–d.

43. Ibid. (90), no. 173.

44. Ibid. (83), no. 140 d–f.

45. The text of Ps. 56 is corrupt in several places, so a division into sections on the basis of formal criteria is very uncertain—an analysis of contents is also problematic for the same reasons. The psalm is (tentatively) divided into the following sections:

vv. 2–3(4), initiated by an exhortation (v. 2a), motivated by _ki_ and perf 3sg×2 (v. 2b–c), while v. 3a, similar in contents to v. 2b–c, has perf 3pl. The _ki_-clause of v. 3b presupposes a preceding command, and the last word of the stanza is unintelligible in its context (cf., however, Michels's attempt at reconstruction, § 36, 23). v. 4 too is textually corrupt, but as the latter part of the stanza displays a second pers sing suffix; v. 4 is, for the time being, collated with vv. 2–3.

v. 5a–b, containing two verbal clauses (perf 1sg, neg impf 1sg); v. 5c has a question—the whole stanza expresses confidence.

vv. 6–7 show (iterative) impfa 3pl (with the exception of v. 7d), giving an account of the activities of a (hostile) third party.

v. 8a is unclear, v. 8b contains an exhortation.

v. 9, addressing YHWH—whether the stanza belongs to the preceding or following section is left open.

vv. 10–11, containing expressions of confidence in different forms.

v. 12a–b, containing two verbal clauses (perf 1sg, neg impf 1sg); v. 12c has a question—the whole stanza expresses confidence.

vv. 13–14 initiated by a nominal clause, followed by modal impf 1sg, motivated in v. 14a by _ki_ and perf 2sg—vv. 14b–c are nominal.

46. Ps. 26 is divided into the following sections:

v. 1, initiated by an exhortation, which is motivated by _ki_ and perf 1sg (v. 1b), followed by perf 1sg and neg impf 1sg (v. 1c–d).

As far as contents are concerned, two different kinds of motivations seem to be used (cf. Kissane, 1953–54: _ad loc._).

vv. 2–3, showing three exhortations (v. 2) motivated by _ki_ and a nominal clause (v. 3a), followed by perf 1sg. As for contents, the exhortations specify those of v. 1—here the motivations are twofold.

vv. 4–8, opened with verbal clauses in neg perf 1sg, followed by neg impf 1sg (v. 4)—v. 5 is similarly constructed. v. 6 displays only impf 1sg(×2), followed in v. 7 by two nominal clauses, while v. 8 has perf 1sg. As for contents, the section seems to specify the utterances of blamelessness in v. 1b: vv. 3–5 describe what the psalmist has not done, vv. 6–8

135

deal with more positive aspects of his conduct. (Note the contrasts שנאתי-אהבתי קהל מרעים-מעון מרעים-מעון, ביתך/משכן כבודך).

vv. 9–11, 12 initiated by a negative command (v. 9), followed by a relative nominal clause (v. 10a) and a verbal clause (v. 10b). v. 11 contains another הלך-clause (cf. v. 1b, 3b)—this time in impf 1sg. The exhortation of v. 9 specifies the contents of the earlier exhortations, v. 10 the behaviour of the third party of vv. 4–5 and 9—against this background v. 11a is understood as modal. v. 11b–c contain further exhortations; v. 12 has perf 1sg, followed by modal impf 1sg, and is supposed to express "Erhörungsgewissheit" (Gunkel, 1926: *ad loc.*).

The psalm contains exhortations in v. 1a, 2, 9, 11b–c, motivations in v. 1b–c, 3–8, and expressions of confidence in v. 1d and 12—these components are all represented and concentrated in v. 1, which is considered the summarizing heading of the psalm.

47. Culley (1967: 39f.), no. 8.

48. Ps. 28 is divided into the following sections:

vv. 1–2, initiated by a description of the invocational situation, followed by a negative command and statements of consequence (v. 1a, 1b, 1c–d). v. 2 contains an exhortation and description of situation (p-vn-s ×2).

vv. 3–4/5 initiated by an exhortation and references to a third party (3), followed by summons to YHWH to take action against them. v. 5, initiated by ki and referring to a third party seems to form the motivation for the preceding exhortations.

vv. 6–7, containing references to first and second person sing. v. 6 is initiated by a "bārūk"-statement (cf. Ps. 31: 22), motivated by ki and perf 3sg (v. 6b), apparently referring to v. 2a. v. 7a contains expressions of confidence, v. 7b shows terminal traits (cf. F 4.2.5).

v. 8, introducing elements not previously found in the psalm: למו could not refer to the third party of vv. 3–6, משיח is new. The stanza is connected to vv. 6–7 through עזי (v. 7)—עז (v. 8).

v. 9 containing exhortations without motivations. The objects are "your people", "your heritage". The stanza is connected with v. 8 through ישועות (v. 8)—הושיע (v. 9).

49. Ps. 61 is divided into the following sections:

vv. 2–3c, initiated by two exhortations (v. 2), followed by a description of situation.

v. 3d–4, containing modal impfa 2sg–s1sg followed by a motivation (ki and perf 2sg).

vv. 5–6a/6b, containing modal impfa 1sg (v. 5), motivated by ki and perf 2sg with first person sing object (v. 6a), and perf 2sg with third person plural object (v. 6b).

vv. 7–8, initiated by modal impf 2sg and introducing a new object (v. 7), followed by modal impf 3sg and modal impf 3pl; both stanzas apparently contain wishes concerning the same person, i.e. the king. The section lacks first person sing references.

v. 9, initiated by ken, followed by cohortative. The "promises" from v. 6 recur in v. 9.

50. Ps. 88 contains *verba cordis* in the perfect in v. 2, 10b and 14a.

v. 2 is followed by modal impf and impv (v. 3) motivated in v. 4 by ki and perf, describing misery; this description is continued in vv. 5–10a (with the exception of v. 9c in the perf); v. 10b and 10c refer to the invocational activity in the perf, and introduce questions, dealing with Sheol-motifs; v. 14a and 14b describe the invocational activity in perf–impf and lead into questions concerning abandonment (v. 15), and later into a description of misery (vv. 16–19, with the exception of v. 16b in the perf).

Formulaic language is present in v. 3a, 3b, 5a, 14a and 15; the similarities of motif and terminology between vv. 3–10 and 14–19 should be noted: תפלה in v. 3 and 14, חמתך-חרוניך in v. 8 and 17, משבריך-מים in v. 8 and 18, הרחקת in v. 9 and 19, מידעי in v. 9 and 18.

The questions of vv. 11–12 and 15 are differently constructed: in the first case with ה(אם), in the second with למה.

136

The observations above lead me to the following tentative division of Ps. 88: vv. 3–10 a, 10 b–13, 14 –19.

51. Culley (1967: 40), no. 9.
52. Ibid. (65), no. 61. Note however that Ps. 26 and 73 do not contain cohortatives.
53. Ibid. (76), no. 108.
54. Ibid. (65), no. 60.
55. Ibid. (56), no. 42.
56. Ps. 22 is divided into the following sections:

vv. 2–3 addressing YHWH—v. 2 contains perf 2sg; v. 3 impf 1sg (קרא cf. F 2.2.1) followed by neg impf 2sg. All suffixes are in the first person sing.

vv. 4–6 lack first person sing references but address YHWH. v. 4 is nominal and opens with c-pr (2sg), vv. 5–6 contain perf 3pl with second pers sing object (with impf 2sg in v. 5 c).

vv. 7–9 describe the situation of the psalmist. v. 7 is nominal and opens with c-pr (1sg), v. 8 contains impf 3pl(×3) with first pers sing object. The change of subject and object of v. 9 is explained if the stanza is understood as part of the exposition of the activity of the previously (vv. 7–8) mentioned third party, i.e. as a quotation.

vv. 10–11, addressing YHWH—v. 10 is nominal, v. 11 a has Hophʿal perf 1sg, v. 11 b is nominal. The section shows first person sing suffixes.

These sections could be labelled "lament" (vv. 2–3), "Beweggrund" (vv. 4–6), "lament" (vv. 7–9), "Beweggrund" (vv. 10–11). To קרא of v. 3 corresponds זעק of v. 6; the quotation of v. 9 becomes the basis for expressions of confidence, initiated by ki, in vv. 10–11. The first lament speaks of abandonment, the second of repudiation; the first "Beweggrund"-section displays בטח pertaining to the experience of the fathers, the second contains בטח relating to the experience of the psalmist. vv. 2–6 are connected to vv. 7–9 through מלט-פלט in v. 5 c, 6 b and 9, through אלי אלי in v. 2 and אלי in v. 11 b, and through the aforesaid בטח-clauses (note also the contrast v. 4 a–v 7 a).

vv. 2–11 will, in the following, be considered as the introduction of the psalm.

vv. 12–17/18–19, initiated by an exhortation, addressed to YHWH (v. 12 a), followed by motivations initiated by ki (v. 12 b–c). The situation of the psalmist is specified in vv. 13–14 (perf 3pl); vv. 15–16 b contain an account of his personal state (perf). In v. 16 c a somewhat surprising impf 2sg–s1sg is found (cf. however Gunkel, 1926: ad loc.)—v. 17, initiated by ki, resumes the description of the third party from vv. 13–14. vv. 18–19 contain references to the personal state of the psalmist (v. 18 a), and to a third party (vv. 18 b–19). Michel (1960: § 23, 31) underlines the modal aspect of the impfa of v. 19.

vv. 20–22 a contain exhortations, addressed to YHWH—the section shows certain terminological similarities to vv. 12–17 (cf. אל תרחק in v. 12 a, 20 a; עזר in v. 12 c, 20 b; ארי in v. 17, אריה in v. 22). vv. 20–22 a lack direct motivations.

v. 22 b: for perf 2/3sg between sections dominated by exhortations and sections containing modal impfa 1sg, cf. G 5.2.4.

vv. 24–25: הלל is found both in v. 23 a and 24 a, but, in contrast to v. 23, v. 24 contains exhortations addressed to three different categories; the motivations follow in v. 25 (ki and perf 3sg).

v. 26: the first part of the stanza addresses YHWH and is terminologically connected with v. 23 b, while the latter part shows modal impf 1sg and picks up the "you who fear YHWH" from v. 24 a (cf. "those who fear him" in v. 26 b).

v. 27, containing modal impfa 3sg, pertaining to "the poor" (cf. "the poor man" in v. 25), and picks up הלל from v. 23, 24 (and 26).

vv. 28–32 entirely lack references to the first person sing, to any of the categories mentioned in vv. 24–25, 26, 27, and do not contain the root הלל. The perspective of the section is wide; here are "the whole earth", "all the families of the nations", etc., here YHWH is described as "the ruler of nations".

57. Culley (1967: 66), no. 63.
58. Ibid. (66), no. 64.
59. Ps. 18 is divided into the following sections:

vv. 2–4, where, in agreement with Schmuttermayr (1971: 33 ff.), I hold ארחמך in v. 2 to be original, and leave the stanza intact. The section constitutes the introit of the psalm in its present form; v. 2 is the outset, and the epithets of v. 3 are a development of חזקי in v. 2, the participle in v. 4 is seen as a concluding apposition and is interpreted together with vv. 2 b–3 (for the discussion of מהלל cf. Schmuttermayr, p. 41 ff.) while v. 4 b–c describe the invocation (for 4 b cf. F 2.2.1); v. 4 c is seen as modal.

vv. 5–6: Stylistically the inversion gives a "Chiasmus in Potenz". Discussing the different aspects Schmuttermayr speaks of clauses "... die sich in Verbalaspekt, Tempus und Modalität nicht von einander unterscheiden" (50 ff.).

v. 7 a–b contain verbal clauses in impf 1sg (אקרא / שׁוע). Michel (1960: § 5, 5) argues that these impfa come from "dem Formular der Danklieder" and must therefore be understood as having "Vergangenheitsbedeutung". However, impf 1sg of *verba cordis* describe a situation of invocation in psalms within the starting group (cf. above) and should be interpreted in the present tense.

v. 7 c–d contain modal impfa. Discussing v. 7 d Schmuttermayr (with Cross-Freedman) states: "Es wird mit zwei Überlieferungen zu rechnen sein ..." (56) so that לפניו and באזניו are variants.

vv. 8–16 contain mainly impfcons 3sg, and lack first person sing references, while vv. 17–18 a show impf 3sg with first pers sing objects. I agree with Michel that the section 6–16 interrupts the themes of v. 7 and 17 "... denn während in vv. 7, 17 das Ich des Beters bestimmend ist, handeln vv. 8–16 nur von Jahwe und den Chaosfluten" (§ 5, 8). For the originality of vv. 8–16 cf. the discussion in Schmuttermayr, p. 116 ff.

vv. 17–18 a, containing modal impfa 3sg (cf. Nyberg, 1952: § 86 p.).

vv. 18 b–19, displaying motivations. For vv. 19 b–20 a cf. Nyberg, § 86 mm.

v. 20 b, containing modal impfa 3sg; v. 20 c, constituting the motivation thereof (ki and perf 3sg).

vv. 21–25, 26–30/31, entirely lacking formulaic language.

vv. 31/32–46 do not contain formulaic language common to psalms within the starting group. For the division of vv. 21–46 cf. Schmuttermayr *ad loc.*

vv. 47–49: v. 47 forms a hymnic opening; the participles of v. 48–49 a are the attributes to the divine name in the preceding stanza. Nouns from the introit are also found here: מפלטי, ישעי + n, צורי.

v. 49 b–c contain impfa 2sg-s1sg and motifs from vv. 31/32–46. For attempts at interpretations cf. Scmuttermayr *ad loc.*

v. 50 For concluding impfa 1sg cf. F 4.2.5.

v. 51 lacks first person sing references. For motif similarities cf. Ps. 28: 8, 61: 7 f.

60. Culley (1967: 90), no. 175.
61. Ibid. (75), no. 104.
62. Ibid. (75), no. 103.
63. Ibid. (78), no. 118.
64. Ibid. (75), no. 105.
65. Ibid. (39), no. 7.
66. Ibid. (40 f.), no. 10.

67. Ibid. (47), no. 24.

68. Note that Ps. 28:1 and 143:7 contain consecutive perf—Culley has not, however, included the initial w̱ᵉ in the system.

69. Culley (1967:88), no. 168.

70. Ibid. (83), no. 140.

# Chapter G

1. Cullley (1967) nos. 34, 35, 38, 39, 53, 55, 56, 57, 120, 121, 122, 124, 129, 136, 138, 139.

2. Ibid. (52), no. 34.

3. Ibid. (52), no. 35.

4. Ibid. (53), no. 38.

5. Ibid. nos. 70, 110, 125, 130, 134, 164, 166, 172, 174, 67, 128, 131, 135.

6. Ibid. (80), no. 126.

7. Ibid. (51), no. 32.

8. Ibid. (52), no. 36.

9. Ibid. (57), no. 44.

10. Ibid. (56), no. 43. Note, however, *impf* 2sg in Ps. 142:8d.

11. Ibid. (67), no. 66.

12. Ibid. (89), no. 171.

13. Ibid. (86), no. 156. Note that the object of Ps. 18:20b–c is in first person sing, while Ps. 22:9c–d has second person sing object.

14. Ibid. (71), no. 84.

15. Ibid. (68), no. 69.

16. Ibid. (70), no. 76.

17. Ibid. (84), no. 146.

18. Ibid. (58), no. 47.

19. The placing of this category under the main heading "Statements about YHWH and his relations to the psalmist" is due to practical considerations rather than to a decided attitude towards the question of the subject of clauses in the imperative.

20. Culley (1967:35f.), no. 1.

21. The text of Ps. 17 is corrupt at several points, so that a division into sections on the basis of formal criteria is very uncertain—an analysis of contents is also problematic on the same grounds.

Exhortations are present in v. 1, 6c–8a and 13; the first two introduce clauses with modal impfa (v. 2, 8b). The section 1–2 lacks a direct motivation—vv. 3–5 contain what seems to be declarations of blamelessness, while vv. 6c–8 and 13 are followed by descriptions of a third party, initiated by min (9–12, 14).

It is uncertain whether vv. 6a–b form the conclusion of the section 1–5 (1–2, 3–5) or the outset of vv. 6c–12—the clauses will here be considered as conclusive: certainly it happens that commands are preceded by descriptions of the situation of invocation, but these generally contain impf 1sg of *verba cordis* (28:1, 30:9a, 142:2—cf. however 88:2, 10b, 14a). Furthermore, there are no equivalents within the starting group (with the possible exception of 116:1b) to the ki̱-clause of v. 6b as initiating exhortations (cf. 142:8d, 109:31, 69:36 for concluding functions). The psalm is concluded by two clauses in the cohortative.

22. Culley (1967:36), no. 2.

23. Ibid. (37), no. 3.

24. Ibid. (37), no. 4.

25. Ibid. (37 f.), no. 5.
26. Ibid. (38), no. 6.
27. Ibid. (41), no. 11.
28. Ibid. (41), no. 12.
29. Ibid. (42), no. 13.
30. Ibid. (42), no. 14.
31. Ibid. (43), no. 15.
32. Ibid. (43), no. 16.
33. Ibid. (44), no. 17.
34. Ibid. (44), no. 18.
35. Ibid. (45), no. 19.
36. Ibid. (45), no. 20.
37. Ibid. (46), no. 21.
38. Ibid. (46 f.), no. 22.
39. Ibid. (47), no. 23.
40. Ibid. (69), no. 73.
41. Ibid. (69), no. 74.
42. Ibid. (69), no. 75.
43. Ibid. (70), no. 77.
44. Ibid. nos. 78, 79, 81, 82, 109, 80, 112.
45. Ibid. (71), no. 83.
46. Ibid. (58), no. 47.

## Chapter H

1. Culley (1967: 74), no. 99.
2. Ibid. (73), no. 92.
3. Ibid. (89), no. 170—the initial verb is, however, interpreted as Hiph'il perf 3sg–s1sg.
4. Ibid. (73), no. 93.
5. Ibid. (54 f.), no. 40.
6. Ibid. (48), no. 25.
7. Ibid. (48), no. 26.
8. Ibid. (49), no. 27.
9. Ibid. (49 f.), no. 28.
10. Ibid. (71), no. 85.
11. Ibid. (72), no. 86.

## Chapter J

1. For the terminology, cf. Hartman (1977), who refers to J. L. Austin (cf. J. O. Urmson, Austin, J. L., Enc. of Philos., 1967: 211–215).
2. Cf. Richter (1971: 132 f.).

## Chapter K

1. For vv. 9–13 cf. above n. F 22.
2. vv. 2, 10 b–c and 14 contain perfa 1sg, which is rare in descriptions of invocational situation (cf. F 4.2.3).

3. i.e. imperatives and modal impfa.

4. For the limitation of sections cf. above notes *ad* chap. F–H.

5. For 25:22 cf. below 3.1.6.2.

6. Cf. also Ps. 18:6–16, which interrupt the themes of v. 7 and 17, and lack first person sing references. The five instances of formulaic language point towards units not included in the starting group (cf. E 1.1)—this may indicate a separate origin for the section.

7. If the למו of v. 8a is taken as a general reference to the people (cf. v. 9), v. 8(–9) would offer an example of combination of motifs one and two (cf. 3.1.6).

8. Becker (1966:36) quotes one of the judgements on the psalm: "Wer Ps. 102:1–12 und v. 13ff. für ein Gedicht ansieht (sic), muss gegen Stil, Sinn und Inhalt vollkommen gleichgültig sein oder den Verf. für geistesgestört halten."

9. Becker (1966:43).

10. Ibid. p. 45.

11. Becker points out the similarities between v. 35 and Ps. 96:11–13, 97:1, 98:7–9 and continues: "Diese Psalmen scheinen den interpretierenden Zusätzen von Ps. 102, Ps. 69 and Ps. 22 sowie Deuteroisaias situationsverwandt zu sein ... Stellen des kosmischen Jubels bei Deuteroisaias sind Is. 42:10–13; 44, 23; 49, 13" (1966:48, n. 66).

12. Ibid. p. 47f.

13. (1966:49ff.).

14. v. 30–32 are translated "Es haben gegessen und gehuldigt alle Mächtigen der Erde; vor ihm werden sich beugen alle, die in den Staub sinken; und der seine Seele nicht am Leben hielt/(dessen) Nachkommenschaft wird ihm dienen. Vom Herrn wird erzählt werden dem kommenden Geschlecht;/man wird verkünden seine (Heils)gerechtigkeit dem Volke, das geboren wird (=dem zukünftigen Geschlecht); Er hat es getan." (Ibid.:49f.).

15. "Wer die Stelle Is. 53, 10 aus dem vierten der Ebed–Jahwe–Lieder nicht auf Israel beziehen will, mag davon absehen." (Ibid.:52).

16. Cf. *app. crit.* BHS *ad loc.*

17. For similar motifs, cf. above n. 11.

18. Is. 38:10–20 and Jon. 2:3–10 also deviate from the basic pattern (cf. above n. F 23, and F 15); Is. 38 contains a minor proportion of formulaic language, while out of eight formulas/formulaic systems in Jon. 2, four lacked comparative material within the starting group, two were found in systems for which no common function in context could be isolated, one differed from the other members of its group concerning function, and only one (v. 5a) showed functional similarities to material from the starting group. Thus neither Is. 38:10–20 nor Jon. 2:3–10 may be offered as examples of compositional convention/tradition.


# Chapter L

1. According to Culley (1967:100), theme and motif are defined in terms of content, and refer to "elements of subject matter or ... ideas repeated in a variable form". The larger form ("theme") consists of a "full scene or description of some sort", the smaller ("motif") is "a smaller group of ideas or details".

2. Engnell characterizes the Ebed YHWH-songs as a "prophetic 'Nachdichtung' from a liturgical collection pertaining to the Annual Festival" (cf. A 2.2)—this implies the conscious application of themes/motifs from a number of psalms to the Servant Songs, and thus the distribution and import of such themes/motifs, if any, must be investigated.

3. Cf. Ps. 55:24.

4. For the different designations of "enemies" cf. G. Braulik (1975: 215 ff.), who refers to O. Keel, Feinde und Gottesleugner (SBM 7), Stuttgart, 1969.

5. The exact import of v. 17 c is obscure—for attempts at interpretation cf. Gunkel (1926: *ad loc.*) *int. al.*

6. For v. 11 c, cf. *app. crit.* BHS *ad loc.* The context favours the translation "misery".

7. For מופת cf. Gunkel (1926: 302).

8. Cf. above n. F 9, 10. This view of the structure of Ps. 116 necessitates an English rendering deviating from that of the Jerusalem Bible.

9. Lindhagen (1950: 265).

# Chapter M

1. My principle of selection has been that "common motifs" ought to contain at least one common major lexical item and/or be found in similar contexts; this method of proceeding does however involve a certain amount of subjectivity.

2. The passages underlined form, according to Culley's index, parts of formulas/formulaic systems or variants thereof.

3. The two are often interdependent and thus a distinction is difficult to uphold.

4. For Ps. 89 in its present form cf. below 2.2.4.

5. Cf. Becker's criticism of the "Scandinavian School" (1966: 18 f.).

6. Ibid. 24 f.

7. Whether these units should be labelled "exilic" or "post-exilic" must be determined from case to case; it should however be observed that all four are devoid of accounts of accomplished salvation and subsequent expressions of confidence and praise.

8. Whereas "grief", "sickness", "enemies", etc., constitute traditional elements in "individual laments" within the Book of Psalms, the "ignominy"-motif originates with Jeremiah, who is apparently considered the "archetypal sufferer" (cf. Gottwald, 1954: 39) by later generations.

9. Cf. Gottwald (1954: 33 f.).

10. v. 7 may be seen as a redactional transition, while v. 32 expresses thoughts strange both to the formulaic psalms and the units showing traces of the literary convention outlined above—if the stanza is not seen as a play upon words (שיר v. 31—שור v. 32, cf. Gunkel, 1926: *ad loc.*) the possibility of an insertion could not be precluded.

11. Cf. Gottwald (1954: 34), discussing the fusion of literary types in exilic times.

12. Whereas the expectations manifested in Is. 40–55 are centered on a specific historical figure, the hope expressed in Pss. 22, 31, etc., is "eschatological" (cf. above) and thus probably articulated in a historical situation which provided no room for "political" speculations.

# WORKS CONSULTED

Becker, J.
1966　*Israel deutet seine Psalmen*. Urform und Neuinterpretation in den Psalmen. Stuttgart: Verlag Katholisches Bibelwerk.
Braulik, G.
1975　*Psalm 40 und der Gottesknecht*. Gesamtherstellung Fränkische Gesellschafts-drückerei, Würzburg; Echter Verlag (=Forschung Zur Bibel, 18).
Coote, R. B.
1976　"The application of the oral theory to Biblical Hebrew literature" in *Semeia* 5: 51–64.
Culley, R. C.
1963　"An Approach to the Problem of Oral Tradition" in *VT* 13: 113–125.
1967　*Oral Formulaic Language in the Biblical Psalms*. Toronto: University of Toronto Press (=Near and Middle East Series, 4).
1976　"Oral Tradition and the OT: Some recent discussion." *Semeia* 5: 1–33.
Eissfeldt, O.
1964　*Einleitung in das Alte Testament*. 3rd ed. rev. Tübingen: J. C. B. Mohr.
Engnell, I.
1945　"Till frågan om Ebed Jahve-sångerna och den lidande Messias hos Deutero-jesaja" in *SEÅ* 10: 31–65.
1962　"Lidande" in *Swedish Biblical Encyclopedia:* 1484 ff. 2nd ed. Stockholm: Esselte AB.
Gesenius, W.
(1909)　*Hebrew Grammar* as edited and enlarged by E. Kautzsch. Second
1910　English edition. Revised in accordance with the twenty-eight German edition by A. E. Cowley. Oxford: Clarendon Press.
Gottwald, N. K.
1954　*Studies in the Book of Lamentations*. London: SCM Press (=Studies in Biblical Theology, 14).
Gunkel, H.
1926　*Die Psalmen*. Göttingen: Vandenhoeck and Ruprecht (=Handkommentar zum AT, 2, 2).
Hartman, L.
1977　"Till frågan om evangeliernas litterära genre." Paper prepared for Kungliga Vetenskapssamhället, Uppsala.
Johnson, A. R.
1955　*Sacral Kingship in Ancient Israel*. Cardiff: University of Wales Press.
Kissane, E.
1953　*The Book of Psalms*. Translated from a critically revised Hebrew Text with a Commentary. Dublin: Richview Press.

143

Kosmala, H.
1964  "Form and Structure in Ancient Hebrew Poetry (A new approach)." in *VT* 14: 423–445.
Kraus, H. J.
1960  *Psalmen*. Neukirchen-Vluyn: Neukirchener Verlag (=Biblischer Kommentar zum AT, XV).
Levin, H.
1937  "Portrait of a Homeric Scholar" in *Classical Journal* XXXII: 259–266.
Lindhagen, C.
1950  *The Servant Motif in the Old Testament*. A Preliminary Study of the 'Ebed Yahweh Problem' in Deutero-Isaiah. Uppsala: Almqvist & Wiksell.
1955  "Ebed Yahve-problemet i svensk exegetik. En översikt." in *SEÅ* 18–19: 32–71.
Lord, A. B.
1954  *Serbocroation Heroic Songs. Vol. I: Novi Pazar: English Translations*. Collected by Milman Parry and translated by A. B. Lord. Cambridge: Harvard University Press.
1965  *The Singer of Tales*. New York: Atheneum (Paperback reprint of a 1960 original).
Michel, D.
1960  *Tempora und Satzstellung in den Psalmen*. Bonn: Bouvier und Co. Verlag (=Abhandlungen zur Evangelischen Theologie, I).
Mowinckel, S.
1962  *The Psalms in Israel's Worship*. Translated by D. R. Ap-Thomas. Oxford: Blackwell.
Nyberg, H. S.
1952  *Hebreisk grammatik*. Stockholm: Almqvist & Wiksell.
1973  "Hiskias Danklied Jes 38, 9–20" in *ASTI* IX: 85–97.
Richter, W.
1971  *Exegese als Literaturwissenschaft*. Entwurf einer alttestamentlichen Literaturtheorie und Methodologie. Göttingen: Wandenhoeck and Ruprecht.
Ringgren, H.
1966  *Israelite Religion*. Philadelphia: Fortress Press.
1967  *The Messiah in the Old Testament*. London: SCM Press (=Studies in Biblical Theology, 18).
Schmuttermayr, G.
1971  *Psalm 18 und 2 Samuel 22*. Studien zu einem Doppeltext. Probleme der Textkritik und Übersetzung und das Psalterium Pianum. München: Kösel-Verlag (=StANT 25).
Wittig, S.
1976  "Theories of formulaic narrative" in *Semeia* 5: 65–91.

296-4
5-15